TEEN ADDICTION

Other Books in the Current Controversies Series:

TEEN ADDICTION

David Bender, *Publisher*
Bruno Leone, *Executive Editor*

Scott Barbour, *Managing Editor*
Brenda Stalcup, *Senior Editor*

Paul A. Winters, *Book Editor*

CURRENT CONTROVERSIES

Cover Photo: © Uniphoto

Library of Congress Cataloging-in-Publication Data

Teen Addiction / Paul A. Winters, book editor.
    p. cm. — (Current controversies)
    Includes bibliographical references and index.
    ISBN 1-56510-535-4 (pbk.).—ISBN 1-56510-536-2 (lib.)
    1. Teenagers—Substance use—United States. 2. Substance abuse—
United States. I. Winters, Paul A., 1965-. II. Series.
    HV4999.Y68T44 1997
    362.29'083—dc20
                                         96-42911
                                              CIP

Contents

in a campaign to teach teenagers that drug use was dangerous and unacceptable. That campaign has since tapered off; at the same time, drug use has increasingly been presented as acceptable in the media and popular culture. Drug use by teenagers has risen accordingly.

Chapter 2: Is Teenage Substance Abuse a Serious Problem?

Yes: Teenage Substance Abuse Is a Serious Problem

The use of methamphetamine (speed) is increasing among teenagers, particularly among young white males in southern California, where the drug is plentiful and inexpensive. Because speed is cheap and easy to manufacture as well as highly addictive, crime experts expect use of the drug to rise as it becomes widely available throughout the United States.

No: Teenage Substance Abuse Is Not a Serious Problem

Chapter 3: How Can Teenage Addiction Be Prevented?

believe that such programs have a backlash effect, leading teenagers to use drugs. These critics advocate the legalization of drugs.

Chapter 4: Can Regulation of Tobacco Marketing Prevent Teenage Addiction to Cigarettes?

Yes: Regulation Can Prevent Teenage Addiction to Cigarettes

No: Regulation Cannot Prevent Teenage Addiction to Cigarettes

Foreword

By definition, controversies are "discussions of questions in which opposing opinions clash" (Webster's Twentieth Century Dictionary Unabridged). Few would deny that controversies are a pervasive part of the human condition and exist on virtually every level of human enterprise. Controversies transpire between individuals and among groups, within nations and between nations. Controversies supply the grist necessary for progress by providing challenges and challengers to the status quo. They also create atmospheres where strife and warfare can flourish. A world without controversies would be a peaceful world; but it also would be, by and large, static and prosaic.

The Series' Purpose

The purpose of the Current Controversies series is to explore many of the social, political, and economic controversies dominating the national and international scenes today. Titles selected for inclusion in the series are highly focused and specific. For example, from the larger category of criminal justice, Current Controversies deals with specific topics such as police brutality, gun control, white collar crime, and others. The debates in Current Controversies also are presented in a useful, timeless fashion. Articles and book excerpts included in each title are selected if they contribute valuable, long-range ideas to the overall debate. And wherever possible, current information is enhanced with historical documents and other relevant materials. Thus, while individual titles are current in focus, every effort is made to ensure that they will not become quickly outdated. Books in the Current Controversies series will remain important resources for librarians, teachers, and students for many years.

In addition to keeping the titles focused and specific, great care is taken in the editorial format of each book in the series. Book introductions and chapter prefaces are offered to provide background material for readers. Chapters are organized around several key questions that are answered with diverse opinions representing all points on the political spectrum. Materials in each chapter include opinions in which authors clearly disagree as well as alternative opinions in which authors may agree on a broader issue but disagree on the possible solutions. In this way, the content of each volume in Current Controversies mirrors the mosaic of opinions encountered in society. Readers will quickly realize that there are many viable answers to these complex issues. By questioning each author's conclusions, students and casual readers can begin to develop the critical thinking skills so important to evaluating opinionated material.

Current Controversies is also ideal for controlled research. Each anthology in the series is composed of primary sources taken from a wide gamut of informational categories including periodicals, newspapers, books, United States and foreign government documents, and the publications of private and public organizations. Readers will find factual support for reports, debates, and research papers covering all areas of important issues. In addition, an annotated table of contents, an index, a book and periodical bibliography, and a list of organizations to contact are included in each book to expedite further research.

Perhaps more than ever before in history, people are confronted with diverse and contradictory information. During the Persian Gulf War, for example, the public was not only treated to minute-to-minute coverage of the war, it was also inundated with critiques of the coverage and countless analyses of the factors motivating U.S. involvement. Being able to sort through the plethora of opinions accompanying today's major issues, and to draw one's own conclusions, can be a complicated and frustrating struggle. It is the editors' hope that Current Controversies will help readers with this struggle.

Introduction

Every year since 1975 researchers from the Institute for Social Research at the University of Michigan, in conjunction with the National Institute on Drug Abuse (NIDA), have conducted the Monitoring the Future survey. The survey asks eighth-, tenth-, and twelfth-grade students whether they have ever used alcohol, tobacco, or drugs and whether they currently abuse these substances. Recent results of the yearly survey show that after declining throughout the 1980s, drug use among teenagers has increased during the 1990s. The survey also reveals that alcohol and tobacco abuse have remained unacceptably high. This state of affairs prompted Health and Human Services secretary Donna Shalala to declare that the entire nineties generation of high school students is at risk for addiction and dependence on drugs, alcohol, and cigarettes. Concerned that a number of today's teens will become drug dependent, many public health officials recommend further study of the causes of teen addiction and the influences on teenagers' use of alcohol, drugs, and tobacco. Teenagers and experts cite a variety of causes of substance abuse and addiction among young people.

One of the causes of teenage addiction most commonly cited by health specialists is the tendency of young people to underestimate the risk of dependence associated with drug experimentation. According to these experts, teenagers on the verge of adulthood are naturally prone to engage in risky behavior. Smoking, drinking, and drug use may seem "adult" to youths who are not mature enough to understand that such behavior poses a threat to their health and well-being, argue the specialists. Many teenagers discover the risks of substance use only after suffering the adverse effects of addiction. Leah, a sixteen-year-old smoker from Washington, D.C., says she did not understand the dangers when she began smoking. She expresses an attitude typical among teens, saying, "When I first started [smoking] I figured, okay, one cigarette is not going to hurt me." Leah admits that she is now addicted, and she confesses that she has tried to quit several times but has been unable to do so.

Compounding teenagers' underestimation of the danger of addiction, according to Lloyd D. Johnston, director of the Monitoring the Future survey, many of today's teens have not been educated about the risks of drugs and addiction. Looking at the survey results over the years, Johnston notes that the decline in drug use during the 1980s coincided with a public health campaign that taught teenagers to "Just Say No" to drugs, alcohol, and tobacco. The demise of that campaign, Johnston contends, is partly responsible for the rising rate of teen substance abuse in the 1990s. He argues that today's teenagers underestimate the dangers of addiction because they have not received drug resistance lessons in schools, seen antidrug commercials on television, or heard warnings against drug use from parents, community leaders, and peers the way young people in the 1980s did. "Teens from a decade ago knew more about drugs," he asserts. Johnston predicts that teenage drug abuse and addiction rates will continue to rise in the absence of effective antidrug messages.

Many public health experts maintain that the risk of addiction is overwhelmingly strong for adolescents and teenagers who experiment with what are called "gateway drugs"—cigarettes, alcohol, and marijuana. According to a 1994 report by the Center on Addiction and Substance Abuse (CASA) at Columbia University in New York City, twelve- to seventeen-year-olds who smoke or drink are very likely to try marijuana. Furthermore, the report's authors assert, the younger children are when they begin to smoke, drink, and experiment with pot, the likelier they are to move on to abuse of cocaine, heroin, and hallucinogens. CASA contends that the recent rise in drug use measured by several national surveys, including the Monitoring the Future survey, portends a future of heavy drug use and likely addiction for many of today's teens. The center's report concludes, "The more often an individual uses any gateway drug . . . the likelier that individual is to become a regular adult user and addict." Among those who might agree with CASA's view is Sabrina F. Hall, a teenager who is a self-described addict and a member of a twelve-step group. Writing in *Newsweek*, she states, "There's no doubt in my mind that cigarettes are a gateway drug. About five months after I started smoking I started doing drugs." Hall's experience with addiction began when she started smoking cigarettes in the fifth grade.

Noting another disturbing trend, Johnston argues that many teens are receiving mixed signals about the use of cigarettes, alcohol, and marijuana from parents and other adults who experimented with drugs during the 1960s. "Today's parents actually used drugs when they were teens and may feel hypocritical telling their own teens not to use," he explains, especially since many of them believe that they suffered no long-term adverse effects. Johnston contends that the lack of parental guidance contributes to the rising rate of teen drug use. Some psychologists agree with Johnston's assessment, maintaining that children and teenagers learn attitudes toward drug abuse and inherit patterns of addiction from their parents. According to George Marcelle, spokesman for the Department of Health and Human Services' Center for Substance Abuse Prevention, "Children who witness adults using alcohol or drugs to cope learn to use it that way." Teenagers whose parents are addicts are more likely to become addicts themselves, health experts argue. On the other hand, almost all agree, parents can also play a strong role in discouraging teenagers from becoming drug abusers and addicts.

Identifying the causes of teen substance use and dependence plays an important role in the prevention of addiction among teenagers. Health experts agree that there are many overlapping causes, ranging from underestimation of the risks by young people to the influence of parents and other adults. Proposed solutions also run the gamut from public health campaigns and education programs to twelve-step programs to drug testing of children by parents. *Teen Addiction: Current Controversies* examines the causes of and proposed solutions to teenage drug use and addiction.

Chapter 1

What Are the Causes of Teenage Addiction?

CURRENT CONTROVERSIES

Chapter Preface

Confronted with the problem of teen addiction, public health experts, parents, and other concerned individuals have long struggled to understand why young people begin using marijuana, alcohol, and other habit-forming substances. In recent years, as public disapproval of smoking has increased, a great deal of attention has been paid to the question of why some teenagers smoke cigarettes.

In a 1994 report, *Preventing Tobacco Use Among Young People*, former U.S. surgeon general Joycelyn Elders examined the reasons teenagers smoke. Elders argues that adolescents are naturally prone to experiment with risky behavior such as smoking and also tend to underestimate the potential for addiction. She maintains that cigarettes are too easily available to minors, who are too young to fully understand the dangers.

Reporter Monika Guttman, who investigated the reasons teens smoke in an August 1995 article in *U.S. News & World Report*, found that peer pressure is one of the primary reasons that teens begin smoking. According to Guttman, many of the teenagers she talked with said that they began smoking in order to fit in with their friends and peers. As "Dimpy," a fourteen-year-old high school student in Santa Monica, California, told Guttman, "All my friends smoke. Once they pressure you, you start."

Many health experts and public policy makers argue that cigarette advertising encourages adolescents to smoke. John P. Pierce, professor of preventive medicine at the University of California, San Diego, maintains that "tobacco marketing is much stronger than peer pressure in getting a youngster to take the first step toward smoking." His research shows that children as young as six years old can identify "Joe Camel," the cartoon character in advertisements for Camel cigarettes. Pierce concludes that cigarette marketing is targeted at a very young audience and that tobacco companies intentionally entice adolescents and teenagers to become smokers.

Experts contend that teenagers smoke because they want to fit in with their peers, because they underestimate the health risks of smoking, because they are manipulated by advertising, or due to a combination of all these factors. The following chapter presents alternative viewpoints from teenagers, community leaders, reporters, and health experts on the causes of teenage substance abuse.

Peer Pressure Causes Teenagers to Smoke

by Steven V. Roberts

About the author: *Steven V. Roberts is a senior writer for* U.S. News & World Report.

Teenagers are the prime target in the tobacco wars. About 1 million start smoking each year—3,000 a day—even though most are too young to buy cigarettes legally. For the tobacco industry, these youngsters are an essential source of new customers. And while cigarette makers deny it, advertising and promotion clearly help attract the attention of teens. The rate of youthful smoking dropped steadily from 1976 until 1984, then leveled off—just as cigarette companies boosted promotional budgets.

The antismoking forces know that an outright ban on cigarettes is impractical and that most of the 46 million Americans who already smoke will not break the habit. So their focus, too, is on teenagers: to keep them from smoking in the first place. Paul Keye, a Los Angeles ad executive who makes antismoking commercials, calls the issue "a war about children." Adds Representative Richard Durbin of Illinois, a leading antitobacco voice: "If we can reduce the number of young smokers, the tobacco companies will be in trouble and they know it."

The Reasons Teenagers Smoke

Reach out—and rebel. As both sides struggle to shape the attitudes and habits of young people, *U.S. News* discussed the smoking issue with twenty teenagers from suburban Baltimore. Half were boys, half girls, and all were between fifteen and seventeen. Over more than four hours of conversation, it became clear that most teens start smoking for two seemingly contradictory reasons: They want to be part of a peer group, while rejecting society and its norms. They want to reach out and to rebel at the same time.

The teens estimate that when they party, 75 to 90 percent of the kids are smoking. "It makes you look like you belong," says Davon Harris, a senior at

Woodlawn High. "For people who are insecure, it's something they have in common with other people," adds a tenth-grade girl. For these youngsters, smoking, drinking and parties go together—a sign that peer pressure is an enormous factor. Most say teens usually smoke in groups, seldom alone. "If you're drinking, you've just got to have a smoke," says Trey Fitzpatrick, a senior at Gilman Academy.

Teenagers also relish smoking as a sign of independence, even impudence. The more authority figures tell them not to smoke, the more psychic rewards they get from the habit. "A lot of people smoke to give the finger to the world," says Trey Fitzpatrick. Adds Joe Katzenberger, a ninth grader at Glen Burnie High: "I think there's some people who want to be bad but without being a criminal."

The young women add that smoking is something to do when they're bored but don't want to eat. And then they get trapped. "People don't stop, because if they do, they're afraid they'll gain weight," says a freshman girl.

Teenagers and Advertising

The big woo. There is no doubt in the minds of these young people that they are being wooed by cigarette advertising. And they say it works—at least some of the time. One brand, Camels, has an appealing youthful pitch and is now running a magazine ad featuring "Joe's Place," a swinging nightspot populated by cartoon characters, all smoking and having a great time. Asked her response to the ad, Julia Beavers, a freshman at Dundalk High, said: "Join the party! Everybody's doing it!" Researchers at the Medical College of Georgia report that almost as many six-year-olds recognize Joe Camel, the brand's standard bearer, as know Mickey Mouse. Scientists at the University of Massachusetts Medical School say 43 percent of the teens they surveyed thought Joe was "cool," but only 1 in 4 adults agreed.

> *"Most teens start smoking for two seemingly contradictory reasons: They want to be part of a peer group, while rejecting society and its norms."*

If Camels appeal to a teenager's desire for acceptance, Marlboros tap his or her impulse to be defiant. Stefanie Albersheim, a junior at Pikesville High, called the Marlboro Man "sexy." Davon Harris looked at a Marlboro ad and interpreted the message: "When you're smoking, you're unstoppable." Michael Eriksen, who heads the Office on Smoking and Health at the Centers for Disease Control and Prevention, says the Marlboro Man "does whatever he wants to do. That appeals to the adolescent who's trying to break away from the rules."

Both brands enhance their appeal by providing coupons in each pack that can be redeemed for hats, jackets and other prizes. Ian Varette, a sophomore at North County High, says one boy he knows is so eager for the merchandise "he'll smoke a couple of packs a day" and steal extra coupons from stores.

These attitudes reinforce the argument of lawmakers who say that one way to curb teenage smoking is to ban cigarette advertising and promotions. But teens are highly skeptical of proposals to raise the legal age for purchasing cigarettes or to increase the price of a pack through higher taxes. "Anyone can get cigarettes now," says Julia Beavers. "It won't change anything." In fact, some teens say, this strategy could backfire: If cigarettes are harder to get, they might become even more desirable.

Another approach that shows little promise: parents and teachers preaching the evils of smoking. Julia Beavers says: "My mother gave me this big old speech—blah, blah, blah—but she smokes." Even the president, the ultimate authority figure, carries little weight. Most of the kids are cynical about the government, and they think politicians are not really serious about reducing smoking, because tobacco taxes bring in so much revenue.

Health Concerns Affect Teenagers

However, these youngsters have been impressed by stark images of the damage caused by smoking. One girl's father, a hospital administrator, gave her photos to take to school comparing the lungs of a smoker and a nonsmoker. The smoker's lungs were "Diet Coke brown" in color and definitely a turnoff. Her conclusion: "Cigarettes kill you inside." A junior boy suggested introducing teens to an older person suffering from smoking-induced cancer: "See this sad sucker; this is what you're going to look like."

But the most effective way to keep kids from smoking is to convince them that it is not cool. The most ardent foes of tobacco in this group find it "disgusting" or "gross," words describing yellowing teeth, foul breath and smoke-stained clothes. One sophomore recalls her first smoke this way: "I remember sitting there and thinking—I was cool, I'm a rebel. Now, I look back, and I was such a dork."

Cigarettes Addict Teenagers and Lead to Use of Other Drugs

by Sabrina F. Hall

About the author: *Sabrina F. Hall is a teenager who is a self-described smoking addict.*

I think cigarette smoking is highly addictive and very expensive. Especially when you're thirteen and get $8 allowance. Right now I'm going to ninth grade and started smoking in sixth. The first cigarette I ever had was in fifth grade. My mom was walking our dogs and found an unopened pack. She brought the cigarettes home and put them by the garden to use as insecticide—a friend in Hawaii had told her that tobacco stops ants from attacking plants.

The First Cigarette

Of course, when I found the pack, I picked them up, being the little rebel I was and, I suppose, still am. I took them to my bedroom, out on my porch and lighted one up with the matches I stole from Dad. I didn't get a buzz, because I didn't inhale, but just the fact I was actually smoking made me think I was cool. But my snobby friend Donna didn't think so. She was just looking at me like I was the stupidest thing on earth. Which I probably was, because I still smoke till this day.

I've tried to quit, but it's very hard when all my friends smoke, too. When I started smoking regularly, in sixth grade, I was in Tilden Middle School. I would say only about twenty people smoked other than me. At the end of the year, at least 200 people were smoking on a regular basis. It was pretty bad. Some kids' grades went down, including mine, from skipping classes to get nicotine in their system to last them through the day. (Pretty pathetic, huh?)

Some people think that Joe Camel is directed toward teenagers. Well, I don't think so. If they are trying to direct it toward teenagers, they are doing a pretty bad job. I'm sorry, but a goofy-looking camel who smokes his brains out doesn't quite turn me on. Actually, I have never seen an ad that made me want to smoke a particular brand. All those cigarette ads are practically the same. They all have beautiful women smoking, acting like they are having the time of their lives. In real life, I know that that model with perfect white teeth doesn't get close to a cigarette.

My parents often ask me, "Where do you buy your cigarettes, anyway?" I buy them anywhere. There are very few places that don't sell me cigarettes. Hardly anyone ever asks me for ID. Maybe I look eighteen; maybe I just put another $2.50 in the cash register. One of the places that do not sell me cigarettes is the Safeway down the street. Last time I went there, I stole four packs of cigarettes, got caught, got arrested and had to write an essay on why stealing is wrong. Man! The lengths addicts go to!

There's no doubt in my mind that cigarettes are a gateway drug. About five months after I started smoking I started doing drugs. I'm in Narcotics Anonymous for marijuana and alcohol abuse. Almost everyone I know, except for three people, started smoking *before* doing drugs. That has to tell you something.

Ignoring the Health Dangers

Since I've started smoking I can hardly run around the block without getting out of breath. A lot of my friends have gotten asthma. My mom and dad quit smoking about fourteen years ago, and my mom now has cancer and my dad has had three heart attacks. My grandma quit eight years ago, and she has emphysema. Not only that—my two grandfathers died from the results of smoking. After all these problems, you'd think I'd know better than to smoke. But I guess I don't.

I can't tell that I smell when I smoke, but my parents and others can. I remember one time, before I smoked, I left my jacket at my friend Brynn's house. Her whole family smoked. I got the jacket back around five months later, and I had to throw it away because it smelled like an ashtray. So I feel sorry for those who don't smoke and have to put up with my odor all day. When I smoke in my room at home, I hang out the window.

> *"There's no doubt in my mind that cigarettes are a gateway drug."*

I've now switched to mentholated cigarettes. For two years I smoked another popular brand, but they made me feel like my breath stunk, so I changed to the mentholated. Now I'm not only addicted to the nicotine, I'm addicted to the menthol too! Yippee!

To kids or teenagers who think smoking is cool or who want to try it, I say, don't! It might calm you down when you're really worked up, but twenty years from now you might find yourself *really* calmed down. You could get emphysema, asthma, lung cancer, throat cancer and much more.

For any parents who have kids who smoke or who are worried that they'll start, the honest truth is you can't do anything about it. You can tell them cigarettes are bad and so forth, but there is nothing else you can do. If you tell your kid not to smoke, your kid might not smoke in or around the house but your kid is sure not going to stay away from smoking when you're not there. So unless you want to lock your kid in the house, there is nothing you can do. All you can do is pray that your kid has the strength to quit. Right now, I don't. I have told my parents that I will try to stop by Christmas as a present to them.

Smoking at Drug Rehabilitation Meetings

Like I said, I belong to Narcotics Anonymous. Similar to Alcoholics Anonymous, it is a 12-step program to give people the strength to stay drug free. I've been clean for more than seven months. I would have been over a year free if I hadn't had a relapse with some friends. It's funny, but I think it's easier to give up drugs than cigarettes. Most of my friends in N.A. feel the same way, I bet. We're permitted to smoke at N.A. meetings, and I know I would rather go to meetings that allow smoking than those that don't.

I really hate the thought of quitting. I hate the thought of never having another cigarette, even though I know how bad they are for my health. I even wrote to Congressman Henry Waxman to say that I would like to testify in Congress about teenage smoking and how many really young kids are hooked bad on cigarettes. But yet, I don't want to do anything that might make cigarettes more expensive to buy or harder to get. I say it's because I don't want to do anything that would make my friends mad at me, but I know that's not the real reason. You see, I'm really hooked on cigarettes. I guess if I wanted to be a real friend to the other kids I would do everything I could to help them kick cigarettes just like they are trying to kick dope. I only know for sure that smoking sucks . . . no ifs, ands or butts.

Teenagers Underestimate the Risk of Addiction

by Richard J. Bonnie and Barbara S. Lynch

About the authors: *Richard J. Bonnie and Barbara S. Lynch were members of the Institute of Medicine's Committee on Preventing Nicotine Addiction in Children and Youths and coedited the committee's report,* Growing Up Tobacco Free: Preventing Nicotine Addiction in Children and Youths.

In the 1990s, it has become disturbingly clear that the remarkable progress made in recent decades in reducing tobacco use has stalled, if not stopped. In 1964, when the surgeon general first raised warnings about the health hazards of cigarettes, 40.4 percent of adults smoked. By 1990, only about 26 percent did. Unfortunately, there it has leveled off. In addition, the use of smokeless tobacco, especially snuff and chewing tobacco, has become a serious problem. But the biggest reason progress in reducing tobacco use is in jeopardy is that young people are smoking about as much as they did a decade and a half ago [in 1980]. Indeed, the number of young tobacco users may be on the rise.

Rates of Smoking Among Youth

According to the University of Michigan's *Monitoring the Future Project*, 29.9 percent of high school seniors smoked regularly (in the last thirty days) in 1993, about the same as in 1980 (30.5 percent). The number of daily smokers was 21.3 percent in 1980 and 19 percent in 1993. Although small increases and decreases have occurred in these rates over the years, a 1.8 percent increase in daily smoking between 1992 and 1993 is statistically significant and therefore of concern. Among eighth-graders, 16.7 percent were regular smokers and 8.3 percent smoked daily in 1993. Overall, more than 3 million children and youths now smoke in the United States, consuming a conservatively estimated 516 million packs of cigarettes annually. A bright spot in this otherwise dim picture has been a dramatic decline in daily smoking among African-American youths, from 16 percent in 1980 to 4.4 percent in 1993. Experts are uncertain about the reasons for this decline.

Abridged from Richard J. Bonnie and Barbara S. Lynch, "Time to Up the Ante in the War on Smoking," *Issues in Science & Technology*, Fall 1994, pp. 33–37. Copyright 1994 by the University of Texas at Dallas, Richardson, Tex. Reprinted with permission.

The use of smokeless tobacco, which was seldom used by adolescents before 1970, has tripled since then. According to the Michigan study, 10.7 percent of high school seniors were using snuff and chewing tobacco in 1993, 3.3 percent of them daily. Among eighteen- to twenty-four-year-old men, the daily rate was 8.2 percent in 1991. Young people consume more than 26 million containers of smokeless tobacco each year.

> *"Overall, more than 3 million children and youths now smoke in the United States."*

It is obvious that the forces propelling the consistent decline in adult smoking have not worked as effectively among the young. Statistics on youths are troubling in that they prefigure a continuing heavy societal burden from tobacco use, especially since surveys indicate that most smokers (about 89 percent) begin between the ages of eleven and eighteen and that nicotine addiction begins during the first few years of tobacco use. More than 400,000 people die prematurely each year from diseases attributable to tobacco use—more than from AIDS, alcohol, car accidents, murders, suicides, drugs, and fires combined. In addition, the Office of Technology Assessment estimated the social costs of smoking—additional health care costs, for instance—at $68 billion a year in 1990. Thus, the nation has a compelling interest in reducing the social burden of tobacco use.

Yet another concern is that just as progress in reducing tobacco use has stalled, aggressive marketing by the tobacco companies has continued to increase. Industry spending on tobacco products hit $4.6 billion in 1991, up 13 percent from 1990. Advertisements inevitably are seen by the young at a susceptible time in their lives. The ubiquitous display of messages promoting tobacco use clearly fosters an environment in which experimentation by youths is expected, if not implicitly encouraged.

To make a substantial and enduring reduction in the prevalence of tobacco use among America's children and youths, aggressive measures are needed. Indeed, public health officials fear that consumption of tobacco will rise unless decisive steps are taken to prevent it. It is time for a national commitment to implement a youth-oriented strategy for preventing nicotine addiction. Such an effort must include greater enforcement of existing federal, state, and local regulations and enactment of strict new ones.

Skewed Choices About Smoking and Health

If adequately informed, adults are assumed to be capable of making rational and voluntary choices that involve weighing the risks and benefits of a particular behavior in light of their own preferences and values. On the question of tobacco use, the critical issue is whether children and adolescents are capable of doing the same. No one argues that preteens have the necessary abilities to make rational choices about tobacco use. Unfortunately, though, a significant number of adult smokers begin using tobacco before becoming teenagers. Data from the 1990 Youth Risk Behavior Survey indicate that 56 percent of youths have tried smoking and 9 percent have become regular smokers by age thirteen.

Some researchers have suggested that adequately informed adolescents (over age thirteen) exhibit cognitive decisionmaking skills similar to those used by young adults (through age twenty-five). Others have claimed that adolescents are well-informed about some specific health risks of tobacco use. But even if these controversial assertions are accurate, they do not show that adolescents can make sound choices about tobacco use. It is also necessary to take into account other faulty beliefs held by adolescents regarding the consequences of tobacco use as well as youthful tendencies to evaluate and weigh risks and benefits within a shortened time frame. Evidence indicates that adolescent decisions to engage in risky behavior, including tobacco use, reflect a distinctive focus on short-term benefits and a tendency to discount long-term risks and to believe that those risks can be controlled by personal choice.

When children and youths begin to use tobacco, they tend to do so for transient reasons closely linked to specific stages in their development—for example, to assert independence and achieve perceived adult status or to establish bonds with peers who use tobacco. Compared with nonsmokers and youths who do not intend to smoke, smokers and likely smokers also tend to exaggerate the social benefit (by overestimating the prevalence and popularity of smoking among peers and adults) and to underestimate the risks (by underestimating the prevalence of negative attitudes toward smoking held by their peers).

Teenagers Dismiss Long-Term Health Risks

Evidence also shows that adolescents who have begun to smoke tend to discount long-term health risks, even though they seem to be aware of the link between tobacco use and various diseases. For example, in 1989, only half of high school seniors who smoked (compared with three-fourths of nonsmokers) reported believing that smoking a pack or more per day is a serious health risk. In addition, although young smokers understand that a lifetime of smoking is dangerous, they also tend to believe that smoking for a few years will not be harmful. Indeed, they do not expect to become lifetime smokers. What they fail to appreciate, of course, is the grip of nicotine addiction.

"Adolescent decisions to engage in risky behavior, including tobacco use, reflect a distinctive focus on short-term benefits."

The University of Michigan's *Monitoring the Future Project* demonstrates adolescents' failure to envision the long-term consequences of decisions to smoke. High school seniors were asked: "Do you think you will be smoking cigarettes five years from now?" Among the occasional smokers (less than one cigarette per day) who replied, 85 percent predicted that they probably or definitely would not be smoking in five years, as did 32 percent of those who smoked one pack per day. However, at the five-year follow-up, of those who had smoked one pack per day as seniors, only 13 percent had quit and 70 percent still smoked one pack or more per day. Of those who smoked occasionally as seniors, only 58 percent had quit, but 37 percent had actually increased their cigarette consumption.

If a youth decides to begin smoking at the age of twelve or thirteen, the deficit in his or her ability to appreciate the long-term risks of doing so is even more pronounced, and more disturbing, than it is at sixteen or seventeen. Indeed, it is clear that nicotine addiction is most powerful and enduring for youths who begin smoking at the youngest ages. Unfortunately, the age of onset of tobacco use has decreased significantly over the past twenty years, especially for girls.

Efforts to Quit Smoking

Many youths already regret their decision to start smoking and report difficulty quitting even during adolescence. The 1989 Teenage Attitudes and Practices Survey data show that 74 percent of twelve- to eighteen-year-old smokers reported that they had seriously thought about quitting, 64 percent had tried, and 49 percent had tried to quit in the previous six months. Among high school seniors in the years 1985 to 1989, 43 percent of those who had smoked at all in the past thirty days reported a desire to stop smoking. Of this group, and of the subgroup who smoked daily, 28 percent and 39 percent, respectively, stated that they had tried unsuccessfully to stop. In the 1991 Youth Risk and Behavior Survey of more than 12,000 adolescents in grades nine to twelve, a majority of self-reported smokers (54 percent of boys and 62 percent of girls) reported that they had tried to quit smoking in the previous six months.

In sum, when children and adolescents begin to use tobacco, they put their health at risk without a sound understanding of the long-term consequences. They simply do not appreciate the personal relevance of the long-term statistical risks of multiple diseases, and they suffer from a profound inability to understand the power of nicotine. These risk-perception deficiencies as well as tendencies to exaggerate the social benefits of using tobacco justify concerted action to prevent children and youths from starting to use tobacco.

Cigarette Advertising Promotes Teenage Smoking

by Stuart M. Lane

About the author: *Stuart M. Lane is an adjunct professor of pharmaceutical marketing and health care administration at Long Island University in New York.*

> *Smoking is a custom loathsome to the eye, hateful to the nose, harmful to the brain, and dangerous to the lungs.*
>
> King James I, 1604

Almost four centuries ago, the reigning King of England and Scotland felt obligated to protect the well-being of his people by alerting them to the harmful effects of tobacco. Unfortunately, in the United States today, our government abdicates this responsibility to the merchants of this "loathsome . . . hateful . . . harmful . . . dangerous" habit. Tobacco companies use the media to make dubious pronouncements about the advantages of smoking. Children and minors are particularly susceptible to the underhanded tactics used by the tobacco companies. These "nicotine dealers" seek to ensure that a new generation of addicts joins the epidemic numbers of existing tobacco users.

Tobacco Companies Misrepresent the Hazards of Smoking

Until recently, the nicotine industry maintained that their products are not hazardous. Today, while the tobacco companies play down the risks of smoking, they claim that consumers are duly warned of the risks. Cigarette advertisements, however, consistently use language and images which contradict health warnings and the scientific evidence that smoking is hazardous to human health. Adolescents are attracted by the lifestyles of the athletic, young models in cigarette ads. These advertisements create false impressions of the safety and desirability of smoking.

Reprinted, with permission, from Stuart M. Lane, *Marketing Cigarettes to Kids*, a publication of the American Council on Science and Health, 1995 Broadway, 2nd Floor, New York, NY 10023-5860.

Smoking is a hot topic. There are heated debates and pending lawsuits over the responsibility of the nicotine industry in alerting consumers to the harmful effects of tobacco products. Recently, much concern centers on the apparent targeting of children for the massive promotional campaigns of tobacco companies. The Tobacco Institute, the well-financed trade and lobbying organization of the nicotine industry, "updated" its public relations campaign with the stated intention of dissuading minors from smoking and restricting children's access to tobacco products. However, recent studies confirm that these specific advertising and promotional programs do not dissuade young people from smoking. Rather, they target this age group and actually encourage youth to start smoking and to become addicted to nicotine.

The nicotine industry has a long history of using deceptive practices to increase tobacco revenues. It is necessary to penetrate this "smoke screen" to understand, as clearly stated by a U.S. District Judge in a lawsuit against cigarette manufacturers, "Who are these persons who knowingly and secretly decide to put the buying public at risk solely for the purpose of making profits, and who believe that illness and death are an appropriate cost of their own prosperity?"

This guide to the nicotine industry and its marketing tactics will clarify *Facts & Fallacies* about tobacco advertising and promotion. . . .

Hooked on Nicotine—The Next Generation of Addicts

FALLACY: The tobacco industry does not need to encourage young people to smoke. It can thrive on the existing number of nicotine addicts.

FACT: Since smoking causes a half million deaths each year, and other smokers die from natural causes or quit, tobacco companies need to addict young smokers to sustain the profits of the nicotine industry.

In this country alone, the tobacco industry must attract nearly two million new smokers each year to replace those who quit or die prematurely. Most of these replacement smokers are children or adolescents: approximately 60 percent of smokers start by age thirteen and 90 percent by age nineteen. Almost 5,000 children and teenagers need to be addicted to nicotine every day simply to maintain the size of the smoking population.

> *"Tobacco companies need to addict young smokers to sustain the profits of the nicotine industry."*

Since children begin smoking at an average age of thirteen years, tobacco addiction is a childhood disease. To protect children from its harmful effects, forty-six states and the District of Columbia have passed legislation that outlaws the sale of tobacco to minors. Nevertheless, according to current estimates, more than three million youths under age eighteen consume 947 million packs of cigarettes and 26 million containers of smokeless tobacco per year, accounting for illegal sales of $1.26 billion and profits of $221 million in 1988.

Although most adolescents are aware that smoking is a health hazard, few believe that it is a threat to their personal health. Adolescents also greatly under-estimate the addictive nature of smoking. Young smokers, like other addicts, rapidly become dependent on and lose control over tobacco use. Over half of high school seniors who smoke are unable to quit. While only 5 percent of these students believe they will still be smoking five years after graduation, in fact more than 70 percent are still smoking eight years later.

> *"Children addicted to nicotine frequently become lifelong consumers of tobacco products."*

Children addicted to nicotine frequently become lifelong consumers of tobacco products. Indeed, almost half of smokers born since 1935 started before age eighteen and have since contributed to the long-term profits of tobacco companies. Because 90 percent of new smokers today begin by age nineteen, tobacco industry profits now and in the future largely depend on attracting these "most important customers"—children.

The tobacco industry knows that most adults who smoke were children who could not quit.

The Ban on Television Advertising

FALLACY: The tobacco industry's ability to market its products has been greatly limited since the ban on televised advertising.

FACT: Since the television ban of tobacco advertising more than twenty years ago, cigarette companies and their brands have been promoted to youth through other media . . . and are still seen on television.

By the time radio and television ads were discontinued in 1971, tobacco companies had already shifted their advertising and promotional expenditures to other categories. Initially, billions of dollars went into print media, so that today cigarette manufacturers are the single largest group of advertisers in newspapers and magazines in the United States. Cigarettes are also the most heavily advertised product on billboards.

To illustrate the extent to which cigarettes are advertised, a 1986 Federal Trade Commission report showed that the amount of money spent to promote cigarettes between 1975 and 1983 increased from $490 million to $1.9 billion. By 1988, this amount increased to $3.26 billion (nearly $9 million per day). This increase greatly exceeds inflation.

Over the years, the nicotine industry steadily increased expenditures on promotional activities to "make new friends and influence people" to smoke. Many of the promotional materials for cigarettes, such as non-tobacco products bearing cigarette brand names (e.g., lighters), do not show the Surgeon General's health warnings that are required on print ads.

Tobacco company sponsorship of sporting events and stadium billboards across the country allow cigarette brand names to be shown or mentioned on television or radio to young audiences, despite the ban on broadcast advertising. *Marlboro* cigarettes received several million dollars of advertising exposure at the Indianapolis 500, the most widely watched auto race in the country. Not surprisingly, Philip Morris is one of the top ten corporate donors in the United States, with donations totaling over $40 million in 1992.

According to the Tobacco Institute's own *Cigarette Advertising and Promotion Code of Ethics*, the tobacco industry cannot directly recruit celebrities to endorse smoking. However, cigarette companies discovered an effective way to circumvent this rule: covert advertising in movies. Until this practice was exposed, cigarette manufacturers paid movie makers to include smoking scenes and use their products in films. For example, Philip Morris paid the producers of *Superman II* to feature *Marlboro* cigarettes more than two dozen times in the movie. The film's audience consisted primarily of young viewers who were targeted for this pro-smoking message. Overt funding of movies has since stopped, but when films such as *Superman II* are shown on television or played on VCRs, they deliver pro-smoking messages to millions of young viewers in the United States and around the world.

History has shown that, unless restrained, tobacco companies will continue the deceptive use of media to sell disease and death to young people.

The Selling of Disease and Death in the United States

FALLACY: The tobacco industry does not advertise and promote cigarettes to children.

FACT: The marketing strategies of cigarette companies are designed to attract youth to become regular tobacco users.

The Tobacco Institute and other agents of the nicotine industry continue to insist that advertising and promotion serve primarily to retain cigarette brand loyalty, not to increase the consumption of tobacco. The industry contends that they are not trying to recruit new, young nicotine addicts.

> *"Tobacco company sponsorship of sporting events . . . allow[s] cigarette brand names to be shown or mentioned on television or radio to young audiences."*

The absurdity of this claim can be proven by simple mathematics. Cigarettes have one of the most tenacious brand loyalties of any consumer product. Fewer than 10 percent of smokers switch brands in any one year. Given that cigarette companies spent $3.6 billion on advertising and promotion in 1989, $900 would have been spent on each one of the four million smokers who switched. The average consumer, however, spent slightly less than that amount on cigarette purchases. Tobacco advertising and promotion are economically rational only if the industry attracts new young smokers or discourages current

31

smokers from quitting. Furthermore, many companies own a number of brands. (For example, R.J. Reynolds owns *Camel, Winston, Now, More* and *Doral*.) If smokers switch from one brand to another owned by the same company, there would be little effect on profit.

Tobacco companies currently invest $4 billion annually in cigarette advertising and promotion. Tobacco industry leaders may want us to believe that this $4 billion advertising campaign does not persuade anyone to smoke. Media executives surely think otherwise. As related by the former chairman of one of the world's largest advertising agencies, "I am always amused by the suggestion that advertising, a

> *"The marketing strategies of cigarette companies are designed to attract youth to become regular tobacco users."*

function that has been shown to increase consumption of virtually every other product, somehow miraculously fails to work for tobacco products."

The Tobacco Institute, however, still claims that the industry does not encourage young people to smoke. The Institute points to the voluntary *Cigarette Advertising and Promotion Code of Ethics* as a defense of the cigarette industry. The code says that models in advertisements shall appear to be over twenty-five years old. The ads should also not suggest that the models' attractiveness and good health are due to smoking or that they have just participated in "physical activity requiring stamina or athletic conditioning beyond that of normal recreation."

Images of Smoking in Ads Aimed at Teenagers

Questioning the actual effect of these tobacco industry guidelines on children, a seventh-grade student surveyed classmates on the magazines that they read, the cigarette advertisements in those magazines and the students' knowledge of the harmful effects of smoking. Only a third of the students knew that a half million Americans die every year from smoking related causes. This figure is more than twice the total number of deaths in the United States due to alcohol, car accidents, fires, AIDS, illegal drugs, suicide and homicide combined.

Regardless of their intended audience, cigarette ads appeared frequently in the magazines that students read most often, *Sports Illustrated* and *People*. Moreover, the students thought that the cigarette ads made smoking look glamorous, healthy and youthful. These images directly contradict the industry's own "ethical" advertisement policies.

Cigarette advertisements appear in many publications teenagers read, particularly those featuring sports, celebrities and attractive lifestyles. The prime example, *TV Guide*, receives more cigarette advertising revenue than any other magazine—$36 million in 1985—and reaches almost nine million adolescents twelve to seventeen years old.

R.J. Reynolds Tobacco Company was the exclusive sponsor of *Moviegoer* and

Movies U.S.A., two youth-oriented magazines given away free of charge at movie theaters across the country. *Tobacco and Youth Reporter*, a publication of the nonprofit organization STAT (Stop Teenage Addiction to Tobacco), revealed that these customized, single-sponsor magazines included several full-page advertisements for *Camel* and *Salem* cigarettes. There were no other ads. Obviously, R.J. Reynolds felt it was important to target their brands at youthful and image conscious consumers. Forty percent of all movie audiences are under age twenty-one, and teenagers go to the movies more frequently than adults.

> *"Cigarette advertisements appear in many publications teenagers read."*

The tobacco industry gives away samples of its products to hook young people. The industry promotes tobacco with coupons. Frequently, adolescents receive free cigarettes at rock music concerts and sporting events. By distributing samples of fruit-flavored smokeless tobacco, the industry encourages the addiction of larger numbers of children to nicotine. These activities occur in spite of the Tobacco Institute's rules against offering free samples to people under age twenty-one or within two blocks of schools, college campuses or playgrounds.

Candy cigarettes are a favorite of many children and help promote cigarette brand labels. Marketing toys resembling cigarette packs and lighters is another common practice. These products, although not manufactured by the tobacco industry, remain on the market despite obvious trademark infringement. Cigarette companies conveniently look the other way because having their brand names on candy and toys render cigarettes more innocuous among other commonly acceptable consumer goods. Children learn at an early age to associate tobacco products with the more enjoyable things in life: food, music and fun.

Joe Camel—Public Enemy #1

The most blatant example of marketing tobacco products to children is the *Joe Camel* campaign. In 1988, R.J. Reynolds, the manufacturer of *Camel* cigarettes, launched its "smooth character" advertising campaign. The central player of the promotion is a cartoon camel, *Old Joe*, modeled after such characters as James Bond and the actor Don Johnson of television's *Miami Vice*. Ads feature the cartoon character in all the "in places," accompanied by beautiful women, race cars and jet planes. Joe Camel always has a cigarette at hand, illustrating that smoking is an essential part of this youthful and glamorous lifestyle.

Many tobacco industry analysts and public health workers believe that the goal of this campaign is to reposition *Camel* cigarettes to compete with the Philip Morris brand *Marlboro* for the illegal children's segment of the U.S. tobacco market. (*Marlboro* has been the most popular starter cigarette for years, but *Joe Camel* apparently jumped ahead of the *Marlboro Man* in today's youth targeted marketplace.) Indeed, *Old Joe Camel* ads and promotional offerings for posters, T-shirts, baseball caps, etc. appeared in magazines widely read by teenagers, including *National Lampoon, Rolling Stone* and *Sports Illustrated*.

One of the most appalling ads in decades—the "beach rape"—is clearly sexist and promotes male violence against women in the name of "smooth moves." The ad implicitly offers an inducement to under-age boys to redeem a coupon to obtain a free pack of *Camel* cigarettes (so that they can "impress" women). When confronted by a U.S. congressman, the Chairman of R.J. Reynolds belittled the ad's offensive aspects by describing it as taking a "humorous approach." The stated intention of the campaign, according to this tobacco company representative, was not to offend anyone or encourage minors to smoke. However, there is little humor in luring young men, or the women they are being urged to impress, to nicotine addiction, disease and untimely death.

Nevertheless, the "smooth moves" *Camel* campaign fulfills the best hopes of R.J. Reynolds and the worst fears of those concerned with children's health. Three studies published in the *Journal of the American Medical Association* (December 11, 1991) clearly demonstrated that *Old Joe Camel* is recognized and remembered by children as young as three to six years old and affects the smoking habits of over one million teenagers.

In just three years, the illegal sales of *Camel* cigarettes to minors increased from about $6 million in 1987 to $476 million in 1990. During that time, R.J. Reynolds increased its share of the youth market from less than 1 percent to about 33 percent. As a result, **illegal** *Camel* sales accounted for 25 percent of **all** *Camel* sales.

Because of the impact on childhood nicotine addiction and its long-range health consequences, the U.S. Surgeon General and the American Medical Association jointly demanded the discontinuation of the *Joe Camel* character in all advertising and promotions. True to form, R.J. Reynolds rejected the demand and stated, "No linkage has been made between advertising and the consumption of cigarette products."

Tobacco companies claim that they do not intend to market to children. However, their intentions are irrelevant if their advertising affects what children know. It is obvious that R.J. Reynolds is effective in reaching children with *Joe Camel*. The direct consequence of marketing cigarettes to children is the increased consumption of tobacco, which constitutes an important health risk for children.

Industry Efforts to Discourage Teenage Smoking

FALLACY: The Tobacco Institute's public relations campaign is a sincere effort to dissuade minors from smoking.

FACT: The Tobacco Institute's public relations campaign to discourage smoking by minors is a "smoke screen" to protect the nicotine industry's freedom to sell cigarettes to kids.

In December 1990, the Tobacco Institute lobby in Washington announced a $10 million campaign to show lawmakers that the nicotine industry is serious about dissuading young people from smoking. Their program endorsed a national legal minimum smoking age of eighteen. In addition, the Institute calls for adult supervision of cigarette vending machines and adherence to state laws prohibiting the sale of cigarettes to minors.

In reality, the aim of the program is to prevent the legal age for smoking to be raised to twenty-one—at least thirty-nine states already have a minimum age of eighteen or older. Many health organizations, including the American Medical Association and Stop Teenage Addiction to Tobacco, support raising the legal age to twenty-one based on the success of reducing teenage drinking by raising the legal drinking age. Even more important is the fact that all laws supported by the industry would preempt local efforts—such as those by groups like STAT—which have proved effective.

> *"The very fact that tobacco companies encourage youth to decide about smoking should be condemned."*

The tobacco industry's probable ulterior motive in calling for the supervision of cigarette vending machines is to forestall rapidly spreading state legislation which prohibits these machines altogether.

The Tobacco Institute offers informational material and warning signs to retail stores which sell tobacco to remind them and minors to comply with local age restrictions. There is little likelihood that this will have much of an effect. Very few vendors were fined for violating these laws in the past, while almost one billion packs of cigarettes were sold to minors in 1992. Recently, the Teenage Attitudes and Practices Survey (TAPS) illustrated how ineffective the existing measures are at reducing illegal tobacco sales. The study evaluated minors' access to cigarettes and found that under-aged youth were successful in 70 to 100 percent of attempts to purchase their own tobacco. Small stores and gas stations accounted for the majority of illegal cigarette sales. Thus, if local governments don't enforce these legal-age laws, illegal tobacco sales will undoubtedly continue.

Industry Education Campaigns Encourage Smoking

The Tobacco Institute also distributes free to schools and parents a guidebook, *Helping Youth Say No to Tobacco*, to demonstrate the industry's commitment to education. This guide is an obvious fraud and pro-smoking subterfuge. There is no mention of the fact, based on scientific evidence, that smoking is the leading preventable, premature cause of disease, disability and death in the United States. The words nicotine, addiction, heart disease or cancer never appear. Instead, the reader is told: "Young people are aware of the *claim* that smoking presents risks to one's health." (*emphasis added*)

The booklet emphasizes that smoking is a pleasure that adults choose to enjoy. "However, young people are not experienced enough to use the information available to formulate their own decisions. That's why decisions regarding smoking and other adult activities such as drinking and sexual activity, should be made as an adult." The tobacco industry is clearly suggesting to children and adolescents that they can declare themselves grown-up and mature by smoking: Smoking is carefully identified as "adult." The very fact that tobacco companies encourage youth to decide about smoking should be condemned.

Lastly, the booklet fails to address the responsibility of parents as important role models. Neither does it address the effects of second-hand smoke on the health of the children of smokers. For example, a study in the *New England Journal of Medicine* (June 4, 1992) indicates that exposure to tobacco smoke is associated with higher rates of childhood asthma.

American tobacco companies are skillful in cloaking a known harmful product in images and language that appeal to youth. They prey on adolescent insecurity, eagerness for role models and need for acceptance. Advertising can provide images of smoking that reinforce the habit very powerfully. According to Louis W. Sullivan, M.D., former U.S. Secretary of Health and Human Services, "Access to cigarettes is still too easy for those who are under the legal age, and the tobacco industry continues to advertise in a shameful manner to susceptible young people."

Teenagers Are No Longer Taught to Resist Drugs

by Daniel R. Levine

About the author: *Daniel R. Levine is the Washington bureau senior editor of* Reader's Digest.

Author's note: Names of the teen-agers in this viewpoint have been changed to protect their privacy.

Eighteen-year-old Mike Woods of suburban Cleveland describes his schedule this way: Every day after school he smokes marijuana. Then he takes a nap or calls a few friends and just "hangs out." Before he started smoking pot three years ago, his grade point average was 3.5, and he was a star sprinter on the track team. Now his GPA is 2.7, and he has dropped track.

"Pot makes you lazy," says Woods. "I don't like to do schoolwork." Even so, he admits he'll continue smoking marijuana. It has also led Woods and his friends to experiment with stronger drugs. "A lot of people move on to acid," he says. When asked how many other students smoke pot, he laughs. "I couldn't count, it's so many. And it's like that at all the other high schools around here."

Widespread Drug Use

• At an Austin, Texas, music festival, the smell of marijuana permeates the air, and a cloud of smoke hangs thick near the stage. Pipes and joints are passed around freely.

Many of the 14,000 fans wander among the concession stands, most of which are selling pot-related products. Displayed at one stand are Phillies Blunt cigars. Some people buy these, hollow them out and fill them with marijuana. Four teen-age girls finger some herbal cigarettes on sale next to the cigars and ask whether they would get high by smoking them. When told "no," one of the teens responds, "Why would you smoke it if it didn't do anything?"

• In Seattle on a sunny Saturday afternoon, two teens walk past the Westlake shopping center. When I approach the pair with questions, they laughingly admit they are on their way to get high. Three blocks later, we stop on the sidewalk. One of them, Jamie Rogers, pulls a joint from a pack of cigarettes, lights it and takes a deep drag. "There isn't a day that I'm not stoned," he says. "Weed is as common as school lunch."

After declining steadily through the 1980s, teen-age drug use, especially of marijuana, has jumped sharply. Daily use among eighth-graders has *quadrupled* since 1992, according to University of Michigan's Institute for Social Research. In 1995, nearly twice as many teen-agers had smoked marijuana at least once during the previous 12 months as in 1992. Half of high-school seniors have used illegal drugs at least once. And drug use is not limited to marginal students or troublemakers. Says Monica Lobo, a 16-year-old junior from West Des Moines, Iowa: "So many people at my high school smoke pot that you can't even label one group 'the stoners' anymore."

Marijuana is the overwhelming drug of choice among our children, but inhalants—breathable chemical vapors from common household products that produce "psychoactive," mind-altering effects—are also being abused. Twenty percent of eighth-graders admit trying them to get high.

Other drugs being used by teens: LSD and PCP, powerful hallucinogens that can cause prolonged psychotic reactions after being ingested; Rohypnol, also called "roofie," a sedative stronger than Valium; and MDMA, or "Ecstasy," which produces feelings of euphoria. In a recent survey of 12- to 17-year-olds, more than half said heroin and cocaine were readily available.

Teens Are Not Getting an Anti-Drug Message

The reason for this upsurge is increasingly clear, says Dr. Robert DuPont, first director of the National Institute on Drug Abuse. For 13 years, marijuana use dropped because an unrelenting, unified chorus of parents, schools, the media and national leaders made sure teens understood that drugs, starting with marijuana, were dangerous and unacceptable. Then teens began hearing fewer of these messages. Says Susan Acorn, 17, of Omaha: "Nobody talks about it anymore. It's like the subject of drugs is taboo." Meanwhile, popular culture, especially music, has portrayed marijuana as a normal, even glamorous, aspect of teen life. As the Washington *Post* commented last May: "Pot is hip." Drug use began to climb.

"Marijuana use dropped [in the 1980s] because . . . teens understood that drugs, starting with marijuana, were dangerous and unacceptable."

To better understand why, talk with former teen-agers who did get the message on drugs. One success story is Britt Tunick, 23, a graduate student at American University in Washington, D.C. An outgoing brunette, Tunick graduated from high school in 1990 and never used drugs as a teen-ager. Asked why she refrained, Tunick mentions the dangers. "There were all those ads on TV," she says. "'Say no the first time and every time.' We all knew the ads by heart. And it was a constant message." There was a clear understanding that drugs were harmful and socially unaccept-able. Students who used drugs "were considered losers who were going nowhere."

During the 1980s, the most effec-tive anti-drug message was First Lady Nancy Reagan's advice "Just

> *"In the early '90s, though, attention moved away from drugs."*

Say No." Presented to a class of Oakland, Calif., elementary-school children in 1985, the slogan fired the nation's conscience. That year there were just 36 community-based substance-abuse coalitions across the nation. By 1989 there were 650.

The focus on drugs also generated a tidal wave of media coverage. When the Partnership for a Drug-Free America (PDFA) was formed in 1986, communica-tions and advertising experts worked together to create anti-drug ads. The na-tion's media donated $2 billion in time and space, making it the largest public service advertising drive in history.

The Effectiveness of Past Anti-Drug Ads

In the late 1980s, commercials like this memorable PDFA ad blanketed the airwaves:

A stern-looking man faces the camera and says, "Is there anyone out there who still isn't clear about what 'doing drugs' does?" Cut to shot of an egg. "This is your brain." Cut to a hot frying pan. "This is drugs." He breaks the egg and drops it into the pan. It sizzles loudly and fries almost immediately. "This is your brain on drugs. Any questions?"

Television advertising has demonstrated that it can play a powerful role in shaping teens' perceptions of drugs. Last year researchers at The Johns Hop-kins Children's Center studied the effect of anti-drug TV messages on some 700 middle- and high-school students: 97 percent reported that the ads con-vinced them using drugs was "more dangerous" than they had thought; 71 per-cent said the ads would persuade them not to try drugs in the first place.

In the early '90s, though, attention moved away from drugs. In 1989, 518 drug stories were aired on the evening news of the three major networks. By 1994, there were just 78. The number of PDFA spots is down 20 percent since 1990. More important, today's PDFA ads are being scheduled by TV stations during off-peak hours—when young people are less likely to be watching.

Political leaders also focused their attention elsewhere. Says Herbert D. Kleber, executive vice president of the Center on Addiction and Substance Abuse at Columbia University: "This Administration and Congress have really ignored the drug issue."

Chapter 1

The Pro–Drug Legalization Campaign

At the same time, a pro-drug message is emerging as an increasingly influential lobby promotes radical alternative policies such as legalizing marijuana and heroin. One of these outfits, the Drug Policy Foundation, calls itself a think tank on drug policy reform and is backed by George Soros, one of the world's wealthiest financiers. Through his Open Society Institute, Soros has donated over $8 million to the 20,000-member Drug Policy Foundation and other groups.

Soros, who refused *Reader's Digest*'s request for an interview, says through his spokesman that he "has no position on drug policy." Pressed further, the spokesman added that Soros believes "law enforcement has been a failure and decriminalization and legalization should be debated."

On the other hand, the president of the Drug Policy Foundation, Arnold Trebach, admits he is a "flat-out legalizer." At the foundation's annual meeting last October, Trebach presented its highest award and a $6000 check to President Clinton's former Surgeon General, Joycelyn Elders. Elders, who resigned her post after making controversial statements about drugs and sexual behavior, was touted by Trebach as "one of our heroes." She responded with a speech in favor of drug decriminalization. Another of the foundation's awardees was enthusiastically applauded when she exhorted the crowd: "Let's hear it for the junkies!"

The media have also contributed to a pro-drug climate. Last April, ABC television aired the prime-time special "America's War on Drugs: Searching for Solutions." The show put forth "harm reduction," a policy that is supposed to reduce the social and health risks of drug use through such measures as distributing clean needles to addicts.

> *"A pro-drug message is emerging as an increasingly influential lobby promotes . . . legalizing marijuana and heroin."*

In August 1994, MTV aired an hour-long news special entitled "Straight Dope" in which marijuana use was put on a par with drinking coffee or smoking cigarettes. As part of its Cable in the Classroom series, MTV distributed tapes of the show to schools around the country.

Drug legalizers often tout "the European model" for relaxing drug enforcement. Throughout the Netherlands, for example, marijuana and hashish are openly sold and consumed in so-called "coffee shops." But the results are increasingly problematic. Dutch adolescent marijuana use, for example, nearly tripled between 1984 and 1992, while the flow of drugs into bordering countries has grown. At the same time the Netherlands is ranked No. 1 in Europe for forcible assaults, up 65 percent since 1985.

Legalization of hard drugs has produced similar results. In 1989, the Swiss city of Zurich instituted a harm-reduction program that allowed the use and sale of drugs in a downtown park. It was quickly dubbed "Needle Park" because addicts were given free needles, condoms, medical care, counseling and the opportunity for treatment. The number of regular drug users in the park swelled from a few hundred to thousands. By 1992 the operation had to be shut down because of a sharp rise in drug-related violence and deaths. Today, Switzerland is left with Europe's highest per-capita rate of drug addiction and second highest rate of HIV infection.

"Legalized marijuana in the United States would be a disaster," says Columbia's Kleber. "It would create a pediatric epidemic for which we would pay a dreadful price in terms of more damaged children and more damaged adults when they grow up."

Rock Musicians Promote Drug Use

The youthful drug epidemic is further fueled through popular culture, especially by rock music. At the Lollapalooza music festival last July in Great Woods, Mass., the mostly white, suburban teen crowd cheered wildly when rap group Cypress Hill pushed a six-foot-tall "bong," or water pipe, onstage. The group has sold five million copies of its first two albums, one of which included songs titled "Legalize It," "Hits From the Bong" and "I Wanna Get High."

Popular rock star Tom Petty regularly glamorizes marijuana use in concerts and songs. Petty's latest top-selling album includes the lyrics "Let's get to the point. Let's roll another joint." In another he sings, "It's good to get high and never come down."

In a recent study of 12- to 17-year-olds conducted for Columbia's Center on Addiction and Substance Abuse, 76 percent said that the entertainment industry encourages illegal drug use. Phil Cannon, 16, and Steve Logan, 16, both of Broken Arrow, Okla., agree. Cannon started smoking pot when he was 13, and Logan started more than a year ago. They now do it "pretty much every day." Cannon has a persistent cough, and Logan admits, "I forget a lot of stuff, like what happened a couple of days ago." Does popular music promote drug use? Says Logan, "All I know is that almost every song you listen to says something about it. It puts it into your mind constantly." Adds Cannon, "When you see the celebrities doing it, it makes it seem okay."

Children even receive pro-drug messages through their computers. On the Internet, they can find step-by-step instructions on how to roll a joint, bake pot brownies or make LSD.

Some marijuana advocates propagate the notion that hemp—another name for the marijuana plant and for the fiber from it—can "save the world." They promote the plant as our "premier renewable natural resource," which

> *"The youthful drug epidemic is further fueled through popular culture, especially by rock music."*

could be used for paper, food, fuel and fiber, and at the same time, according to one pro-marijuana publication, "balance the world's ecosystems and restore the atmosphere's oxygen balance."

Says professor of pharmacology Billy Martin, a leading marijuana researcher at Virginia Commonwealth University, "It's obvious that hemp is a façade to give marijuana a better name." Nevertheless, hemp products, such as wallets, jeans and hats, have proliferated, and their popularity is evident among teens. For example, when German shoe manufacturer Adidas asked young Americans for new athletic-shoe ideas, the result was a shoe made of hemp.

The Dangers of Marijuana Use

Despite all of these pro-drug messages, the fact remains that marijuana is harmful. Studies show that it disrupts short-term memory and hormonal levels. Young women may find their monthly cycle disrupted. Marijuana alters brain function and harms the lungs—one joint has four times more tar than a tobacco cigarette. During a marijuana high, motor skills such as timing, coordination and alertness are diminished.

Marijuana is also a "gateway" drug: few cocaine, LSD or heroin users did not first smoke pot. One reason is that a teen who uses marijuana is more likely to come into contact with users and sellers of harder drugs. A youngster 12 to 17 years old who smokes marijuana is 85 times more likely to use cocaine than one who does not.

Moreover, teen-age marijuana use is linked to criminal behavior. In 1993, 26 percent of all male teens arrested in 12 major cities tested positive for marijuana. In Washington, D.C., 52 percent of arrested juveniles tested positive for marijuana in 1994—up from 6 percent in 1990.

Fred Motley of Spring Valley, N.Y., understands just how dangerous marijuana really is. He was a 12-year-old honor student when he first smoked pot. "I wanted to be accepted by the cool crowd," he says. He started smoking pot only on weekends, but then moved to LSD, cocaine and crack. He grew increasingly belligerent, routinely skipped school and became depressed. In January 1993 he entered a drug treatment program, and for two years he has been trying to put his life back together.

Lloyd D. Johnston, program director of the Institute for Social Research at the University of Michigan, who has tracked teen drug trends since 1975, sees the country in the same position today as it was in the late 1960s when anti-drug attitudes broke down and use skyrocketed. Says Johnston: "This has all the signs of another epidemic. In the last one, thousands of lives were lost and millions adversely affected. We cannot afford another tragedy like that."

Teenagers Learn to Abuse Alcohol from Their Parents

by Felton E. May

About the author: *Felton E. May is a Methodist bishop in Harrisburg, Pennsylvania.*

Editor's note: This viewpoint is excerpted from testimony given by Felton E. May on March 3, 1993, to the President's Commission on Model State Drug Laws.

Our young people also consume alcohol because they see their parents drinking. If mom and dad do it, then it must be all right, despite mom and dad's warnings to the contrary. Alcohol use and abuse is a family affair.

Alcohol Consumption Among Children

Here are some statistics that chill my blood:

• Kids in grades seven through twelve consume 35 percent of the wine coolers sold in the United States.

• 10.6 million children in grades seven through twelve drank more than 1 billion cans of beer in 1991.

• Nearly one out of three high school seniors reported in 1990 that they had consumed five or more drinks at one sitting during the preceding two weeks.

• While the number of young persons who consume alcohol daily has been decreasing during the past decade, in 1990, according to a study on drug use by the University of Michigan's Institute on Social Research, one in four high school seniors admitted drinking some sort of alcoholic product daily.

• Young persons who binge drink (drinking multiple servings of alcohol in a short period of time) skip school twice as frequently as non-drinkers. Binge drinkers are twice as likely to receive C's in school than non-bingers.

In community after community, neighborhood after neighborhood, across the United States, drug addiction very clearly claims more than addicts as its vic-

From Felton E. May's testimony before the President's Commission on Model State Drug Laws, March 31, 1993.

tims. When one or both parents are addicted, their children and other family members become victimized by this insidious disease.

What happens to these children? In thousands of families, grandmothers become mothers again as they assume the primary responsibility for their grandchildren whose parents are addicted or have been killed through some violent act. Without the loving care of these dedicated—but overworked—women, we would be facing even more tragedies of abuse, neglect and even the deaths of these young children.

The toll on these women is *enormous*. According to the US Census Bureau, 3.2 million children in the United States live with their grandparents—an increase of almost 40 percent in the past decade. Systemic issues related to AIDS, legal problems, lost values, miseducation, poverty and substance abuse have caused millions of the elderly to assume important child-rearing responsibilities.

Drug addiction doesn't care if you're African American, European American, Native American, Asian American, or Hispanic American. Addiction doesn't care if you're poor, middle class or rich. Despite this knowledge, drug use is most commonly portrayed as an African-American issue, an inner-city phenomenon involving illegal drugs bought and sold by persons with little money.

Parents Influence Children

Let me give you an example of how this stereotype is just plain wrong. Alcohol is the drug of choice for the vast majority of Americans. In many families, the mothers and fathers don't know what influence their before-dinner martinis are having on their children.

I was in Edmonds, Oklahoma, participating in *Born Free/StayFree*, an excellent drug education/prevention program. . . . During our session with parents from this upper middle class suburb of Oklahoma City, a woman asked how she could get her daughter to obey her orders to not use drugs. She said, "I keep telling her not to drink or use drugs, but she turns to me and says back, 'But you use them every day.'" The mother's response was:

> *"When one or both parents are addicted, their children and other family members become victimized by this insidious disease."*

"I'm the parent. You are the child. I give the orders. What I say is what counts. What I do isn't your business."

This mother was perplexed and in pain. She could not understand how her daughter would react in such a way. "I'm the parent. She's the child. It's none of her business what I do." She asked me for my reaction. I could give her none then, for her addiction had taken over. She couldn't see that her disease was setting up her daughter to become an addict herself. The question was asked, "Will you as this child's mother give up drinking and drug use so that your

44

child will have a healthy role model?" The mother dropped her head and she did not answer. Only tears came forth.

For this family there was hope, because the mother and daughter would at least begin to communicate through their involvement in *BornFree/StayFree*. Most parents and children in addicted and co-dependent situations have not had access to that type of assistance.

The Community as Family

. . . We need to talk about the community as family. We need to talk about the need for each of us to be responsible for our neighbors' well-being, and the consequences if we don't take that responsibility. We must become our neighbor's neighbor.

In Shade Gap, Pennsylvania, a tiny community located about ninety miles west of Harrisburg, members of the community began to overcome their silence, their co-dependence. Their motivation was simple: too many young people were dying because of drug-related causes, and it was clear that drugs were as easy to buy in Shade Gap as in any city.

Meeting in the town's fire hall at the behest of a United Methodist layman, Bill Bair, the community, acting as a family caring for all its members, formed the Shade Gap Drug Task Force. One of the first things the task force did was to develop a "Statement of Support for a Drug-Free Community," and seek commitment from the 147 families in Shade Gap. In that statement, families agreed not to use illegal drugs, to safeguard the use of prescription drugs, and to consider alcohol as a drug. A hotline was created for reporting illegal drug activity and a community education program was developed, with free counseling available.

Of the 147 families in that community, 142 signed the statement. More importantly, to show their commitment publicly, each family placed a sign in their front yard. It's been nearly three years since that first meeting, and the community remains active in this effort. Why? Because persons overcame the co-dependency to begin to understand the disease and face it head on. It was a family taking care of its brothers and sisters.

Teenagers May Try Heroin to Emulate Rock Musicians

by Dennis Cooper

About the author: *Dennis Cooper is a contributing editor of* SPIN, *a monthly music magazine.*

When an Alice In Chains video comes on MTV, most of us either crank the volume, or immediately change channels. But heroin addicts and struggling former addicts hear something in Layne Staley's grade-school junkie poetry that we can't: a kind of siren. As someone who has had several close friends who were strung out on heroin in the past two years, I think I have a sense of how this private call-and-response works, even if I can't understand the mechanisms. According to my friends, just the mention of the word "heroin" in a lyric, or a photograph of a hypodermic on a CD cover, or the sight of junkie musicians all wrapped up in some glamorous video, and they go crazy with longing for the stuff, even when, as in the case of Alice In Chains, they know full well that what they are hearing and seeing is silly and contrived. Recently, I saw one of the most intelligent people I know absolutely freakout watching the old Thompson Twins video "Don't Mess With Doctor Dream." One minute we were guffawing at its cheesy imagery—spinning needles, screaming skulls, sanctimonious antidrug captions—and the next minute he was a jittery wreck begging me to drive him downtown so he could buy a few bags.

Music Videos and Teenage Drug Use

Can I blame MTV? Maybe, at least according to Michigan's Institute for Social Research (ISR). In 1994, it conducted a survey in which 50,000 high school students around the U.S. were asked about drugs. According to the study, drug use is on the rise again. Big surprise. And Dr. Lloyd D. Johnston, program director of ISR, thinks the problem lies in the representation of drug use in contemporary music, films, and rock videos. Like generations of academics before him, he sees teenagers as a kind of intellectually passive, easily

Dennis Cooper, "Junkie See, Junkie Do," *SPIN*, March 1995. Reprinted by permission of Camouflage Associates, New York.

seduced herd in need of strict parental guidance. Never mind that this conclusion is pure speculation, and not based on data actually unearthed by the survey. In this confused world of ours, even the appearance of fact attains a kind of godlike status, and statisticians, those great cultural simplifiers, are considered something on the order of the gods. Thus, when the *New York Times* reported the results of this survey, Johnston's ruminations were treated as though they were the story, and the teens' statements were lost in the shuffle. It's all spurious, but coming on the heels of the aforementioned Thompson Twins fiasco it got me to wondering whether Johnston has a point.

Donna Gaines, sociologist and author of *Teenage Wasteland: Suburbia's Dead End Kids*, doesn't think so. She sees youth culture and drug use as historically enmeshed. "With MTV, drug use has just taken on the status of a commodity," she says. "When I was younger and some actress was wearing a really cool miniskirt in a movie, I wanted that miniskirt. Now when you see some guy getting fucked up on MTV, you want to get fucked up. But videos are expressive rather than coercive. I don't see it as a causal relationship. Anyway, most hard-core drug users don't watch MTV. Its audience is mainstream. And I don't think it's such a great cultural force anyway. Maybe for twelve-year-olds."

MTV's Antidrug Policy

Video director Samuel Bayer, who has worked with Nirvana and Hole among others, gives MTV more credit, but thinks the network is sufficiently prudent in its policies. "I grew up in the '70s, when there were drug references all over the place," he says. "Kids are smart enough to read between the lines. Something like Kurt Cobain dying [the lead singer of Nirvana committed suicide in April 1994]—that's what happens when your life is fucked up. If anything, videos have the opposite effect."

In the same *New York Times* article that reported Johnston's findings, Carole Robinson, a senior vice president at MTV, said that the network's guidelines call for programming that does not "promote, glamorize, or show as socially acceptable the use of illegal drugs or the abuse of legal drugs." And anyone who watches MTV regularly has noticed those little Tinker Bell–like digital blurs clinging to the pot leaves on hip-hop artists' caps. In a Tom Petty video, a line about rolling a joint has been auditorily altered into a nonsensical slur. Especially since Cobain's death, the network's

> *"Just the mention of the word 'heroin' in a lyric, . . . and [addicts] go crazy with longing for the stuff."*

nonmusic programming has been nearly didactic in its cautionary tone regarding hard drug use. Still, you don't need a degree in deconstruction to see the signs of drugginess all over MTV, whether it's Alice In Chains' elegant little travelogues of junkie life, or Ministry's "Just One Fix" clip, in which heroin withdrawal is given a snazzy, action-packed movie-trailer look, or even Tori Amos's clip for "God," in which a character simulates "tying off." If kids are smart enough to know what's fiction and what's not, then they are smart enough to decode these kinds of messages too.

> *"You don't need a degree in deconstruction to see the signs of drugginess all over MTV."*

If MTV has a drug policy, it's a confused one. It is as if the network had chosen to approach drug-related videos the way a makeup artist might approach crow's-feet on an aging actress. Pot leaves, pills, and hypodermic needles are successfully smudged beyond recognition, but the subtleties remain. Maybe this kind of approach works with drugs such as pot, cocaine, and acid, although I doubt it. But heroin is a complicated beast with a very subtle system of signifiers, most of which are invisible to nonusers' eyes. Take the aforementioned Ministry clip. To MTV, it must read as an anti-heroin statement, with a surface narrative in which two young junkies detox in a shabby hotel room, intercut with shots of heroin icon William S. Burroughs waving his hands in a cautionary manner à la the giant alien in *Twin Peaks*. But look closer and there's old Al Jourgensen himself slouched in the hotel's lobby. In one telling close-up, he looks at the camera and rubs his nose with one finger. It's a nervous tic common to junkies, and a signal to knowledgeable viewers that Jourgensen, or rather his character, is loaded on the stuff. So later when the boys leave the hotel, supposedly detoxed and ready for the world, and Jourgensen picks them up hitchhiking, there's a definite subtext, i.e., they'll be shooting up again any minute.

Drug Images in Videos

I happened to catch Primal Scream's "Rocks" video on MTV's *Alternative Nation*. Primal Scream is a U.K. band whose work flaunts the meagerness of its members' imagination and technical ability. Its records are affectionate pastiches of other, more talented bands' music, past and present. It's all very postmodern. In its current incarnation, Primal Scream is pretending to be junkie rock. Keith Richards, Johnny Thunders, and Gram Parsons are the obvious models. In 1994, the band even caused a little scandal in the British rock music press by jokingly referring to the late River Phoenix as a "lightweight" [the actor died of a drug overdose in February 1994]. In the "Rocks" clip, frontman Bobby Gillespie stumbles around slurring about the joys of unmitigated hedonism. His hair is long and filthy, his skin has the hue of a corpse, and his mouth hangs partway open in an imitation of someone nodding out on his feet. I think you're supposed to be bemused. But all I could think about while watching this freak show was what my troubled friend would do when he saw him.

Because heroin withdrawal is such an agonizing process, and the recovery period so long and psychologically disruptive, it doesn't take much to make former addicts slip. Heroin may be a nasty business on a day-to-day basis, but the drug's immediate effect is profoundly pleasurable. My friends say it is like the ultimate orgasm, elongated and unattached to the rest of the world. Its intensity, they tell me, makes life's relatively sober comforts like friendship, romance, and sex seem petty. So reentering the world in which these things are generally held as sacred can feel, I'm told, like a compromise, especially in the first year or so, when your body's gradual reconstruction causes almost continual discomfort. Thus even something like Kurt Cobain's suicide, which most of us interpret as the ultimate anti-heroin statement, has a double meaning. For instance, the morning I heard the news, I phoned up a Nirvana fan I knew who was struggling to stay off dope, and begged her to please fucking quit before she ends up like him. "No," she said, her voice edgy with a hunger and anger I couldn't decode. "You don't understand." And she explained how Cobain's inability to stay clean only reinforced her feeling that sobriety wasn't worth the trouble. When I hung up the phone I knew she was going to run out and score. And she did.

Musicians' Influence on Teenagers

When I was a young teen listening to the Velvet Underground and John Lennon's "Cold Turkey," and reading William S. Burroughs and Alex Trocchi, I never—and I think I can include my former friends in this—thought, "Hey, I should try this heroin stuff." Presumably most kids are the same way now. But a number of young rock fans have started shooting heroin because one or more of their heroes has made light of the subject. I know a handful of them myself. I'm talking about talented, smart people who just want to experience everything that there is to experience. To them, River Phoenix convulsing on the sidewalk, or Kristen Pfaff nodding out in a lukewarm bath [the bass player for the band Hole died of a drug overdose in June 1994]—these things are as faraway, unreal, and mythical as the song lyrics that render heroin use a profound, sensual voyage into the mysteries of the self. Some people will always choose to do extreme things. Others, maybe most of us, will choose to learn by listening to songs about extreme activities, or by reading nonfictional accounts. So how do those of us who don't really understand what it means to shoot heroin tell users to stop what they're doing because it's scaring us? Well, we

> *"A number of young rock fans have started shooting heroin because one or more of their heroes has made light of the subject."*

can't. But we can air our fears and presumptions and hope for the best.

A former member of several prominent alternative rock bands, who requested anonymity, spoke to me about his own confusion around the representation of heroin in videos. A former junkie, he has been clean for several years. "I can see both sides," he says. "When you're doing dope, it permeates everything you do and think. It feels like enlightenment, and you also feel really alone at the same time, so you want to network. It's not even a conscious thing. I can't even watch MTV anymore, it's so full of junkies. I can spot them in an instant, and I feel like they're calling to me from this terrible and fascinating place in my past. The thing is, they're some of the most interesting musicians around, so it would be crazy to shut them up. So it's just this tortuous paradox." So the only option he sees is looking the other way?

Other Options for Fighting the Influence of Drugs

"What other way?" he says. "That's what heroin does, removes you from the scariness in the world. I found out that doesn't work either. If there is an option, it's being strong, and believing in your loved ones. Because everything else, including drugs, is just meaningless entertainment."

Point is, even if MTV could eliminate every shred of every drug reference in every video, it wouldn't make any difference, and it would only cause the network to seem even more untrustworthy than it already is. Why should MTV be self-censorious when the record, television, and film industries are expected to support artistic freedom of expression? Pop culture is a mishmash of images of every type of behavior and attitude. It presents a chaotic, multitudinous portrait of life that becomes a kind of collective truth which we are then responsible for decoding and using according to our own personal needs at any given moment. For every positive portrayal of drug use, you can be sure there's a negative one somewhere else. It's a balance, and that's fine, because, as painful as it may be to watch friends suffer because of some irresponsible rock star's posey bullshit, we have no control over one another's lives. We choose people to love according to psychological systems that are nobody's business but our own. And if we suffer as a consequence of our love, them's the breaks.

Teenagers Use Psychedelics for Excitement and Escape

by Robert B. Millman and Ann Bordwine Beeder

About the authors: *Robert B. Millman is chairman of the Department of Public Health and Ann Bordwine Beeder is an instructor in psychiatry and public health at Cornell University Medical Center in New York City.*

Psychedelics have been used since ancient times in diverse cultures as an integral part of religious or recreational ceremony and ritual. The relationship of LSD and other psychedelics to Western culture dates from the development of the drug in 1938 by the chemist Albert Hoffman. LSD and naturally occurring psychedelics such as mescaline and psilocybin have been associated in modern times with a society that rejected conventional values and sought transcendent meaning and spirituality in the use of drugs and the association with other users. During the 1960s the psychedelics were most often used by individuals or small groups on an intermittent basis to "celebrate" an event or to participate in a quest for spiritual or cultural values.

Current Patterns of Psychedelic Drug Use

Current use varies from the rare, perhaps once yearly episode to enhance a party, concert, or holiday to frequent use by people who may use the drug to seek solace in an altered state that is free of the pressures of consensual reality such as school or social obligations. LSD has been used compulsively by some young people as self-medication of psychopathology such as unwanted thoughts and feelings. For clinicians to best treat patients using hallucinogens, a basic understanding of the patterns of use and settings where the drugs are used is essential.

Hallucinogens and psychedelics are terms used to describe both the naturally occurring and synthetic compounds primarily derived from indoles and substituted phenethylamines that induce changes in thought or perception. The most frequently used naturally occurring substances in this class include mescaline

Excerpted from Robert B. Millman and Ann Bordwine Beeder, "The New Psychedelic Culture: LSD, Ecstasy, 'Rave' Parties, and the Grateful Dead," *Psychiatric Annals*, vol. 24, no. 3, March 1994, p. 155.

from the peyote plant, psilocybin from "magic mushrooms," and ayuahauscu (yagé), a root indigenous to South America. The synthetic drugs most frequently used are MDMA ("Ecstasy"), PCP (phencyclidine), and ketamine. Hundreds of analogs of these compounds are known to exist. Some of these obscure compounds have been termed "designer drugs."

Perceptual distortions induced by hallucinogen use are remarkably variable and dependent on the influence of set and setting. Time has been described as "standing still" by people

> *"The 'rave' phenomenon has been a major element in the resurgence of psychedelic drug use in Western society."*

who spend long periods contemplating perceptual, visual, or auditory stimuli. Users often describe effects reminiscent of derealization and depersonalization; a sense of enlightenment is common such as a vision of "clear light" at peak moments.

MDMA or "Ecstasy" that is currently in vogue is a synthetic substituted phenethylamine, similar to mescaline, DOM, and MDA. MDMA is a short-acting drug that produces fewer perceptual phenomena and thought disturbances, and less emotional liability [instability] and feeling of depersonalization. Users of MDMA generally do not experience significant visual illusions or the experience of profound cessation of the temporal flow.

Patented by Merck in 1914, MDMA has been widely studied. Ecstasy has been described as an "empathogen" because its most profound effect appears to be the experience of intense emotions and the perception that the user is able to experience the emotions of others. Other observations reinforce this description; David Nichols proposed creation of a new chemical class termed "enactogens," from the Greek meaning "touch within." Many also believe MDMA to be a potent aphrodisiac.

Ecstasy Use and the Rave Phenomenon

The use of hallucinogens by indigenous peoples of the Americas is well documented from the arrival of the first European explorers in the late 15th century. Group use in preparation for battle, celebration of particular events, ritual, and healing is typical among many of these tribes. Observers have noted long-standing, culturally integrated use of hallucinogenic plants that is often aimed at the creation of a shared consciousness among participating tribe members. Some accounts suggest that the drug use facilitated entry to an otherwise unavailable spiritual world. Psychedelics in our current culture can be similarly considered.

The "rave" phenomenon has been a major element in the resurgence of psychedelic drug use in Western society. Originating in Europe in the 1980s, raves are parties open to a select public for a fee in a unique location chosen for the night of the event. Major attractions of the rave scene include the unpredictable location and the integral role psychedelic drugs play in the event. Entrepreneurial sponsors, such as club owners, managers, or businessmen within the local entertainment industry rent inexpensive buildings for the event and then spread publicity to attract their audience.

The derivation of the term *rave* might have to do with the loosening of inhibitions and sense of abandon that participants seek incident to the combination of drugs and milieu. The locations play a role in this feeling as they are often warehouses, basements, broken-down condominiums, unused tenements, schools in disrepair, or any other spot that might be conducive to the ephemeral sensibility raves represent.

Participants both bring and buy drugs while listening and dancing to "technomusic" played by disc jockeys. Technomusic dominates the rave culture. The music is marked by a dense, cold beat that enhances the sense of distance and anonymity. Participants attempt to "lose themselves" in the combined effect of drugs and the energetic, rhythmic dancing.

An entry fee is charged at rave parties, ranging from $7 to $20 per person. Because raves are chiefly attended by young people including minors, nonalcoholic beverages are provided, often at inflated prices. The subtext of these gatherings attended by hundreds to thousands of participants involves the surreptitious drug use of the party-goers. Dealers who have drugs for sale often wear characteristic backpacks. Available drugs include LSD, MDMA, and other less potent hallucinogens. Alcohol, marijuana, and cocaine are often less available.

> *"Raves have developed as a situation where young people can experience intense excitement [and] a sense of belonging to a group."*

Participants describe the rave experience as having anticipatory, beginning, middle, and end phases. A person may buy several "hits of acid" and ingest these early on at the party, they may "come on to" the hallucinogenic effects within the first hour, dance furiously for several hours as the drug peaks in two to four hours, "come down" and lay exhausted as the drug effects wane in eight to ten hours.

Dangers of the Rave Experience

Handouts describe the dangers of intensive drug use in these settings and are often distributed at raves by the sponsors. Experience has shown that adverse drug effects may occur in an overheated space where people are dancing vigorously for many hours. The handouts contain specific information regarding the need to drink fluids, take breaks, and leave the scene if paranoia, agitation, or other difficult-to-control symptoms occur.

It might be conjectured that in the modern era, given the very real dangers of intimate sexual contact, raves have developed as a situation where young people can experience intense excitement, a sense of belonging to a group, and escaping from their everyday concerns. It is as if the goal is to depersonalize, to lose oneself in the drug, the group, and the music. . . .

A resurgence of psychedelic drug use is occurring as groups of young people discover the effects of altered associations, perceptual distortion, and heightened emotional states caused by LSD, MDMA, and other hallucinogens. These drugs are widely available, inexpensive, and socially reinforced by various societies of adolescents and young adults. The rave phenomena represent organized and predictable assemblies where a growing movement of young participants engage in psychedelic drug use. Development of rewarding alternatives, including a sense of belonging in "straight" society, is a critical aspect in treating young people involved in these drug-dominated cultures.

Chapter 2

Is Teenage Substance Abuse a Serious Problem?

Chapter Preface

The Monitoring the Future survey, conducted by researchers at the University of Michigan every year since 1975, measures the extent of drug, alcohol, and tobacco use among high school students as well as students' attitudes toward drug abuse. The results of these surveys show that in the 1990s teenagers' use of drugs (most notably marijuana) has increased, while disapproval of drug abuse has declined—a reversal of the trends of the 1980s. The surveys reveal that the percentage of high school seniors who smoke marijuana once a month increased from 11.9 percent in 1992 to 21.2 percent in 1995. At the same time, the proportion of teenagers who perceive marijuana use to be risky decreased from 79 percent in 1992 to 60.8 percent in 1995.

Many health and public policy experts find such survey results troubling. According to Alan I. Leshner, director of the National Institute on Drug Abuse (NIDA), the decrease in the perceived harmfulness of smoking marijuana is most worrisome because this perception is driving the increase in use of the drug. Leshner and others maintain that the effects of smoking marijuana are particularly harmful to high schoolers. Peter Provet, director of adolescent programs for Phoenix House, an addiction treatment facility in New York, reports that teenagers who smoke pot suffer serious psychological problems. "When abused severely, [marijuana] creates paranoia and reduces motivation for all kinds of activities, be it school or sports," he states. Leshner believes that marijuana use would again decline if teenagers were accurately informed about the risks.

However, a significant number of health specialists maintain that the increase in marijuana use among teenagers does not represent a serious problem. They point out that the percentage of high school students using drugs is still far below the peak levels of the late 1970s. Furthermore, some experts, including John P. Morgan, a professor of pharmacology at City University of New York Medical School, argue that high school students are correct to believe that smoking marijuana is not risky. Morgan notes that there are no scientific studies proving that chronic marijuana use has any harmful effects. Lester Grinspoon, a psychiatrist at Harvard Medical School, contends that the parents of many of today's teenagers smoked marijuana in their youth and suffered no long-term harmful effects.

Regardless of whether marijuana is truly harmful, Lloyd D. Johnston, lead investigator of the Monitoring the Future survey, predicts, "As long as we are seeing erosions in the dangers youngsters believe to be associated with these drugs, . . . I expect that we will see a continuation of the increase in drug use." The viewpoints in the following chapter debate whether the use of drugs, tobacco, and alcohol by teenagers is a serious problem.

56

Teenage Substance Abuse Is a Serious Problem

by Donna E. Shalala

About the author: *Donna E. Shalala is the secretary of Health and Human Services.*

At the release of the past two Monitoring the Future surveys [in 1993 and 1994], we have sounded alarm bells about rising levels of substance abuse by American teenagers.

A Renewed Alarm

Today, I want to ring that alarm bell faster and louder and send a message to every parent in this country: Your children are at risk. We have a generation at risk.

The Monitoring the Future survey shows that over the last year [1994–95], teenage tobacco and drug use continued to climb, and alcohol use—while level—remains unacceptably high.

Let me be clear: Use levels have not returned to the peak levels of the 1970s and 1980s, but the trends for marijuana and cigarette use are unmistakably headed the wrong way.

Home by home, block by block, community by community, we need renewed intensity in the war against drugs and children's tobacco use. We need parents and grandparents, siblings and teachers, clergy and coaches, business and government, the media and the entertainment industry—all working together.

We need a broad national effort to reach young people and give them safe passage through the teenage years or else, in a few years, we're going to find ourselves right back where we were in the old days—when children and teenagers viewed drug, alcohol, and tobacco use as perfectly normal and accepted behavior.

Today, as a part of National Drunk and Drugged Driving Prevention Month—proclaimed by President Bill Clinton—Americans all across the country are

Donna E. Shalala, "Remarks by Donna E. Shalala, Secretary of Health and Human Services, at the Monitoring the Future Surveys Press Conference, Washington, D.C.," *HHS News*, December 15, 1995.

turning on their headlights to symbolize the need to keep impaired drivers off our roads.

In that spirit, I want to issue a challenge to all parents and all caring adults—including those who experimented with drugs when younger.

To America's parents, I say, "All of you should be concerned about the findings we are releasing today—and I hope your concern translates into frank talk around kitchen tables all across this country."

"Use the holiday season to gather your families together. Sit your children down. Set them straight about the dangers of drugs, alcohol, and tobacco."

"The myth is that children won't listen to you. The reality is that there's nobody who influences them more than you."

"Government has a strong role to play. We will help you. But nothing can take the place of your love, your concern, and your values."

Teen Smoking

Now, I'd like to talk in more detail about the survey.

The tobacco increases show that the national concern about children's smoking is warranted.

From 1994 to 1995, the percentage of high school seniors who smoked within the last thirty days increased from about 31 percent to more than 33 percent—and the percentage of seniors who smoked daily jumped from more than 19 percent to nearly 22 percent.

Smoking among tenth graders also continued to climb: Nearly 28 percent of our fifteen- and sixteen-year-olds report smoking in the past month, up from more than 25 percent—and the percentage of tenth graders who report daily smoking increased from about 14 percent to more than 16 percent in 1995. Among the youngest members of our survey—eighth graders who may be as young as thirteen—daily and past month smoking has also increased between 1991 and 1995.

"Your children are at risk. We have a generation at risk."

This is a four-year trend of increased smoking among American youth—a trend that in the long run will cost this country thousands of precious lives and billions of dollars in health costs.

The tobacco numbers also show that an American success story is beginning to erode: In recent years, we have been able to report a lower percentage of African-American youth using tobacco than other American teenagers.

That is still true—but the Monitoring the Future survey shows that we are losing ground fast among eighth, tenth, and twelfth grade African-Americans—in all categories of tobacco use. For example, past month tobacco use by African-American tenth graders jumped to 11.5 percent in 1995—almost double the rate from four years ago.

Make no mistake, tobacco use is a pediatric disease: It is an American tragedy affecting all of us.

That's why the president has proposed the boldest initiative in American history to prevent children's smoking—and this survey shows the wisdom of his leadership.

Teen Drug Use

Moreover, the survey's findings on teenage drug and alcohol use underscore the importance of the president's determined leadership in *that* area.

Though illicit drug use among young people is far below the peak levels of the 1970s and 1980s, it is still far too high.

The survey shows that 39 percent of high school seniors reported using an illicit drug at least once in the past year—up from 35.8 percent in 1994. And, for the third consecutive year, we found increases in the percentage of tenth and twelfth graders using marijuana within the past year.

These marijuana increases are particularly significant and they are tied to the increasing perception among young people that these substances are not harmful.

For example, we found a sharp decline in the percentage of eighth, tenth, and twelfth graders who believed there was a "great risk" in trying marijuana.

No wonder. Marijuana continues to be glorified in popular culture as a "soft drug." That couldn't be further from the truth.

"Make no mistake, tobacco use is a pediatric disease: It is an American tragedy affecting all of us."

Our research at the National Institute on Drug Abuse (NIDA) shows that marijuana damages short-term memory, distorts perception, impairs judgment and complex motor skills, alters the heart rate, can lead to severe anxiety, and can cause paranoia and lethargy.

Its use by young people is disproportionately associated with increased truancy, poor school performance, and crime.

These are the facts, which our children need to hear from all of us—especially those who know them the best and love them the most: parents, grandparents, older siblings, and other family members.

Government Efforts to Reduce Teen Drug Abuse

After seeing 1994's increase in marijuana usage, at the Department of Health and Human Services (HHS) we stepped up our efforts to help parents protect their children from the resurgence of marijuana.

We increased our marijuana research agenda at NIDA. We designed new materials for parents and teenagers to promote discussions about marijuana around the kitchen table. We worked with the Partnership for a Drug Free America and other drug prevention groups to develop public service announcements (PSAs) targeted directly at marijuana.

In fact, I just taped a new set of radio PSAs for parents that provide an information hotline where they can get drug prevention resources.

These steps are valuable—and we will increase them—but government action alone cannot change children's behavior, or anybody else's. I wish it could.

Instead, it's going to take every single one of us, locking arms and challenging young Americans to be hooked on hope and too strong for wrong.

The Clinton administration stands side by side with parents in the great moral task of helping the future of our country make safe passages into young adulthood.

> *"Marijuana continues to be glorified in popular culture as a 'soft drug.' That couldn't be further from the truth."*

That's why we proposed the Children's Tobacco Initiative—to ensure that children get their information about tobacco products from their parents and other caring adults—not Joe Camel.

That's why, to stop drug use, we have a tough, comprehensive anti-drug strategy that is working on all fronts—everything from interdiction to more police on the streets to a powerful commitment to prevention.

At the Department of Health and Human Services, this means leading a major research agenda to understand the effects of all drugs and the best prevention and treatment strategies.

It means creating partnerships with hundreds of community groups that have teamed up with more than 30,000 local businesses and non-profits.

It means working with the media and entertainment industries to promote programming that de-glamorizes drug use and other risky behaviors.

And it means sending the strongest possible signals all across the country that we will never, ever support the legalization of marijuana. . . .

Our bold approach is the right way—the common sense way—to help families and save futures.

Do Not Cut Drug Fighting Funds

Unfortunately, there are some in Congress who disagree.

They want nothing less than to retreat on our commitment to the health and well-being of *all* young people—our nation's future and most precious resource.

This is not—I repeat—*not* the time to cut hundreds of millions of dollars for substance abuse initiatives.

This is not the time to slash HHS prevention and treatment efforts—and curtail the leadership that the Substance Abuse and Mental Health Services Administration has brought to this fight.

This is not the time for drastic cuts in the Safe and Drug Free Schools program, a program that helps some 23 million students.

This is not the time to pull back—as the Republican budget is doing—when the monsters of drugs, tobacco, and alcohol are reaching out their long arms to snatch away our young people, their health, and their lives.

Our job as policymakers, as parents, as teachers, as employers, as clergy, and as members of the media is to be the long arm of life and health.

Our job is to keep sending a clear and consistent message to young people: "It is illegal, dangerous, and wrong for you to use tobacco, alcohol, and illicit drugs."

Everywhere our young people turn, they must see and hear that message: Where they live and where they work, where they study and where they hang out.

It must be loud and clear. It must be a steady drumbeat. It must come from parents and older siblings and other family members. And it must come from all of us.

Monitoring the Future is a call to action: It says to parents: "Your future is now, and your future is at risk." We must roll up our sleeves and go to work—and get the job done.

Drug Abuse Among Teenagers Is Increasing

by Peter Wilkinson

About the author: *Peter Wilkinson is a contributing editor of* Rolling Stone *magazine.*

Today, as they have since 1967, young people in San Francisco who get too far into drugs climb unsteadily up the wooden steps of the Haight-Ashbury Free Clinics. On the third floor of 409 Clayton Street, they find a tall, absent-minded fellow blinking behind a pile of medical journals and lab reports—Dr. David Smith, the clinics' founder.

Evidence of a New Wave of Drug Use

"We're starting to see another upswing in drug use," Smith says wearily one recent afternoon. "And another whole new generation is experimenting with hallucinogens." In the clinic hospital were three adolescents who'd been smoking marijuana compulsively. "They'd become dependent on it in relation to every function—to enhance the taste of food, before sex, to listen to music," says Smith. The outpatient roster includes a young man who flipped out on ten hits of ecstasy, another whose head is still buzzing weeks after eating too much acid.

Smith, who describes himself as an advocate of drug decriminalization but not outright legalization, prepared for the next assault by gathering intelligence. On the street a few steps from his office, dealers are already hawking two new drugs: LSD-49, an acid variety, and GHB, an amino-acid concoction that has a mood-altering effect at high dosages. Clinic operatives leave to buy some of both for analysis. Smith looks worried. GHB taken with ecstasy could cause episodes of psychosis. "Kids today," Smith says, "are using themselves as experimental laboratories for strange drug combinations that no scientist ever thought of."

In the stacks on the doctor's desk lie the most recent government surveys: the official numbers on teen drug use. How those numbers suddenly have people talking. It started in spring 1993 with the release of the annual Monitoring the

Future Survey, which is sponsored by research grants from the National Institute on Drug Abuse. The study, conducted by the University of Michigan at Ann Arbor since 1975, was expanded in 1991 to include eighth- and tenth-graders. Now some 50,000 secondary schoolers are polled every year.

The University of Michigan report, the most widely cited of teen surveys, confirmed what many observers had suspected—teen drug use, after falling off for years, was on the increase. One alarming piece of information was that more eighth-graders—thirteen- and fourteen-year-old kids—are using drugs: 15 percent more with regard to marijuana, 30 percent with cocaine.

We do not have a new epidemic, the experts say. What we do have are clear signs that the salutary effects of drug education have worn off. Having watched fewer cautionary filmstrips and heard fewer of the firsthand horror stories that shook up previous generations, the youngest teen-agers are becoming fearless again. "Perceived risk has drifted downward," says Dr. Lloyd Johnston, the principal investigator on the study. Among academics the phenomenon is called generational forgetting.

In January 1994 more data issued from Ann Arbor reinforcing the trend. The official statistics this time showed continuing increases in the use of acid, grass and inhalants—a particularly alarming piece of news. Kids call it huffing—inhaling highly toxic household products like solvents, glues and aerosols. The study revealed that in 1993 one in every nine eight-graders admitted to huffing at least once.

The Wide Availability of Drugs

Wherever David Smith goes these days—on his rounds along the sun-dappled streets of the Haight or to oversee the Rock Medicine tent, which provides free medical service at California rock concerts, he sees pretty much the same thing. The users of glamorous new drugs like GHB exist on the fringe, as do the down-and-out huffers. The great majority of kids who are doing drugs, according to Smith and other experts, are smoking pot and discovering psychedelics.

Walk through any Cypress Hill, Dr. Dre, or Black Crowes show. The smoke smells richer, more potent. And it is. Customers expect high-THC marijuana (tetrahydrocannabinol, or THC, is the psychoactive ingredient in marijuana)—"kind bud" on the concert circuit, "tasty bud" or "purple hair" around the area of Northern California where it is cultivated, or the "chronic" in urban areas. These various hybrid superweeds are grown all over the country, not just in California. THC levels, according to Smith, are ten times higher than what they were for most pot in the '60s.

> *"The official statistics [show] continuing increases in the use of acid, grass and inhalants."*

Domenico, an eighteen-year-old from suburban New Jersey who used to deal drugs in clubs in New York City, started smoking weed at thirteen and quickly graduated to blunts—cheap, hollowed-out cigars filled with powerful grass. "Pot isn't considered as harmful as other drugs," he says. "It's thought of like alcohol—not a big deal. Everybody smokes: Deadheads, geeks, even the GQs—the pretty boys. It can't kill you."

This view isn't unknown in the think-tank community. Dr. Peter Reuter, director of the drug-policy research center at the Rand Corp., in Washington, says that one of the explanations of the upward trend in pot use "is that our prevention messages about marijuana aren't particularly credible. I mean, it's not a very dangerous drug."

> *"Marijuana is a negative social lubricant that fosters . . . risky behaviors."*

Not so, says Peter Provet, director of adolescent programs and clinical support services at Phoenix House, the residential treatment center based in New York City. He sees pot as a pox on the adolescent world. "Marijuana use can have very serious consequences: lack of interest in studies, in goals, then involvement in illegal activity and dangerous behaviors like unsafe sex and violence," Provet says. "Marijuana is a negative social lubricant that fosters these risky behaviors."

The Effect of Drugs on the Young

Research on the effects of marijuana use for kids is ongoing and incomplete. What's known is this: Some temporary muddying of short-term memory can occur with even occasional use, and there may be a risk of bronchitis. Though doctors suspect heavy pot smoking might lead to lung cancer, there's no hard evidence, and with stronger strains, stoners are probably actually smoking *less*. And any direct evidence that pot causes brain damage in humans is still lacking.

Smokers of high-THC weed, however, especially inexperienced smokers, like eighth-graders, do occasionally suffer panic reactions; whether it's from the pot itself or from having heard about overstated dangers is not clear.

"They become very anxious," says Dr. Larry Chait, an independent researcher formerly with the University of Chicago who has been studying marijuana's effects on human behavior for ten years. "They think they're dying or they're going to have a heart attack. This usually clears up in an hour or two. It's scary.

"Younger children, at eighth-grade level and below, are at greater risk," Chait continues, "because their personalities haven't developed well enough, and they aren't mature enough to know how to handle altered states of consciousness. As with any drug, the younger the age of first use, the higher the risk."

The same is true with LSD, in Smith's view. "The younger you are," he says, "the more likely you are to impair your psychosocial development and have adverse reactions." These dangers, however, aren't stopping many kids. Some 6.8 percent of high-school seniors reported having used LSD last year [1993], the highest level since 1985. Among eighth-graders polled last year, 3.5 percent reported having used LSD at least once, up from 2.7 percent two years ago [in 1991], a small but significant blip, say drug educators.

Reasons for the Resurgence of Drug Use

Part of the reason for acid's new infiltration is public relations. Coke and crack caused so much visible destruction in the '80s and hurt so many people so awfully that the two eclipsed the rap on acid. Acid was dropped from the standard high-school-counselor speech, and even the government eased off. The Drug Enforcement Administration (DEA) hasn't busted a major San Francisco acid lab in ten years.

Acid's resurgence makes sense in the odd, cyclical way the drug world makes sense. To a limited extent, social awareness is making a comeback; some '60s values are being repopularized by the kids of hippie parents. Psychedelic experiences are attached to those values. Marketed by word of mouth as a spiritual awakener, acid is again tempting bright young people who are trying to make sense of the world and who want a more intense experience than pot can provide.

"It's considered a more intellectual drug," says Kate Barnhart, who was a peer counselor at Stuyvesant High School, in New York City, before graduating in June 1993. "People read a lot of Beat Generation writers and pride themselves on being out-of-it, genius types. Kids who are into art or music think it makes them more creative."

Like their '60s counterparts, some young users are after some sort of mind expansion. But the fact is a lot of teen-agers today are more interested in acid as a party drug, more as a hedonistic pleasure than a means toward that '60s ideal of an egoless state.

"It feels mightily good, it's cheap, and it lasts," explains Max, who also goes to high school in Manhattan. "The time-per-fucked-up ratio is high."

Another reason—perhaps more pertinent—for the psychedelic rediscovery has been availability and price. California chemists produce blotter acid that sells for as low as $3 a hit. At parties and at concerts, particularly Grateful Dead shows, people often dose one another for free. In high schools across the country, LSD is easy to find.

> *"Part of the reason for acid's new infiltration is public relations."*

Mr. Natural, Mickey Mouse, Black Pyramid, Yin Yang, various Grateful Dead logos and symbols—even Bill Clinton. Every popular variety of acid has a logo and a brand name. Most of the time, LSD is sold as one- to two-centimeters-square paper hits, torn from sheets of easily transportable blotter paper that has been immersed in a solution of acid, alcohol and water. (Think of a page of tiny postage stamps.) Tablets, or "barrels"—saccharin pills that have absorbed 45 to 75 micrograms of the liquefied drug—are also sometimes seen. Gel, or "window pane," looks like a minisquare of plastic. It can be clear or colored.

In all its delivery forms, acid has found a nontraditional home in the rave clubs and a neopsychedelic music scene. At all-night raves, the techno music throbs, lasers split the darkness, and acid is often taken in combination with ecstasy—a powerful hallucinogenic mixture called X&L, or "candy flips," the effect of which is described as an intensified psychedelic trip with a warm, loving edge.

Acid Is Seen as Less Dangerous than Before

From the perspective of the Timothy Leary generation, '90s kids are missing some of the fun—and a lot of the point. Tabs manufactured in the finer labs in the late '60s usually packed 150 to 300 micrograms of LSD, sometimes as many as 500. The idea was to amp up, lose yourself and get as far out into the cosmos as possible. That required 100 micrograms for most people. A lot of the acid sold today is 20 to 80 micrograms, known as "cocktail acid."

Dr. George Gay, with Smith a co-founder of Rock Med for concerts, finds that young people today are generally more cautious in their drug taking. Diluted LSD, Gay says, is made for them. "You're standing there with sweat on your brow, but you're still maintaining. There's a slight edge, distortion of light and sound, some trails, not a profound excursion.

After the government demonized acid in the '60s, the population of new users shrank. Today, most teen-agers, drug counselors say, have no "acid memory." They don't know about flashbacks or suicidal behavior. "High-school seniors have begun to see acid as less dangerous, especially the class of 1992," says Johnston. "Fewer than half thought it was dangerous to try LSD once or twice."

Government agencies and school administrators, meanwhile, have begun to reintegrate LSD into their drug-awareness spiels, while parents, teachers and treatment specialists try to formulate policies that stop just short of chucking offenders out of school. Speaking to dozens of classes every year in California, Smith recommends mandatory family counseling when a kid is discovered holding drugs. "You've got a system that really doesn't believe this happens," he says. "Parents still think drugs are an inner-city phenomenon. And some of them *took* drugs. They believe the phenomenon is over with. But the job of drug education is never done. You constantly have to educate about the facts."

Methamphetamine Use Is Increasing Among Teenagers

by Anthony R. Lovett

About the author: *Anthony R. Lovett is a freelance writer in Los Angeles.*

An hour east of Los Angeles is the San Gabriel Valley, a sprawl of tract homes and minimalls where the big attraction is a theme park called Raging Waters. Out here, far from the smog and crime of downtown, the teen-agers do not care about cocaine, ecstasy or other glamorous drugs of the big city. They prefer getting spun, as they call it, on crystal methamphetamine.

A Methamphetamine Epidemic

And suddenly there's plenty of it around. According to Brenda Heng, an agent with the California Bureau of Narcotics Enforcement (CBNE), amphetamine use is reaching epidemic proportions on the West Coast. "Even crack is not as widespread in this state as methamphetamine," she says. "The market is flooded, so more and more people are doing it."

In 1993, the CBNE seized 360 clandestine meth labs, about 160 more than the federal Drug Enforcement Administration (DEA) seized nationwide. Speed-related emergency-room visits are up; drug counselors are treating a greater number of kids messed up on the drug.

Authorities have attempted to stem this flood of speed not only by imposing tough mandatory minimum sentences but also by classifying certain "precursors"—chemicals essential in the manufacture of methamphetamine—as Schedule II substances. (Drugs are rated under federal law from Schedule I to V in terms of their effects, medical use and potential for abuse.) Ironically, many amphetamines come under the less serious Schedule III.

The federal mandatory minimum sentence for trafficking 10 to 99 grams of meth is five years; for 100 grams or more it's ten years. The feds even target the small-time user. The Anti-Drug Abuse Act of 1988 allows the Department of Justice to ask for a civil penalty of up to $10,000 for illegal possession of small amounts of meth for "personal use."

What brought on the new deluge of methamphetamine? According to sources at the FBI and DEA and local law-enforcement agencies, the organized biker gangs that once controlled the production and distribution of speed from San Diego to Sacramento have in recent years been pushed aside. Now, Mexican nationals are producing export-size quantities of high-grade methamphetamine, some of it in factories located south of the border, where the key ingredient, ephedrine, is not a controlled substance. The rest of the supply seems to be coming from huge, environmentally hazardous labs located in remote areas throughout California.

"The Mexican labs we've seized have far greater production capabilities than the bikers ever dreamed of," says Heng. "And the stuff they're producing is 90 percent pure, which is amazing considering the filthiness of these labs. The bikers could never touch that kind of purity level." The purity is partly responsible for the surge in speed-related emergency-room visits in California. The other prominent factor is the sheer number of new recruits—especially white, male teen-agers.

Speed Is Cheap and Available

Ken, eighteen, works three jobs. He lives in the heart of the San Gabriel Valley, where not too long ago he spent his days and nights getting spun on "oda" (meth) and "just clucking away." Now, Ken says he has stopped using, but with demand as high as it is, he can't resist dealing a little.

Meth is relatively inexpensive to produce, and the current street price is comparable to cocaine's, so meth offers a greater profit margin without the risks of smuggling. Out in the San Gabriel Valley, small-time dealers can pick up an ounce of meth for $600 to $900. On the streets, a gram sells for about $100 for average quality; $150 for "glass," which is extremely pure. The once-popular, less-pure form of speed known as crank is the cheapest of all, but demand has dwindled. "I really don't know anyone who still deals around with that crank shit," says Ken. "Everyone tries for crystal.

"Speed is a really big deal out here, because so many people are making

> *"Amphetamine use is reaching epidemic proportions on the West Coast."*

it," Ken continues. "San Dimas, La Verne, Covina, Glendora are the biggest manufacturers of methamphetamine. There's a lot of cooks around here. They go from hotel to hotel."

And the demand is high, especially for crystal meth, which teen-agers here recently began smoking in glass pipes. The fearless kids of the San Gabriel Valley call it "sucking the glass dick."

Donna Mognett, a licensed psychotherapist in Covina, California, works with teens who have run into trouble with drugs. Mognett calls speed "the most frustrating problem" she has dealt with in twenty years of practice. "We've seen some pretty bizarre behavior and done some serious interventions in my time in order to get through to the patient," says Mognett, "but [speed] doesn't compare. These kids have no response. They're flattened, turned off, pathological. Their thought processes are so skewed, they can't think properly."

Mognett thinks the real culprit here is not the dealer or the manufacturer

> *"Speed is a really big deal out here [in California], because so many people are making it."*

but the user's own low self-esteem. For this, she puts the onus on parents and the school system, both of which Mognett accuses of failing to pose an educational and ethical challenge for young people.

"A lot of these kids are from good families," Mognett says, "and what I see quite often is that they've been given too much freedom. The school day is very short; many students are on the street by 1 in the afternoon."

In his six years of practice at Charter Oak Hospital, in Covina, Dr. Said Jacob has seen a marked increase in white, teen-age, male speed freaks who use the drug "to give them more energy for sports and for sex—especially for sex." Jacob has also noted a decrease in the age of his patients, having treated some regular meth users as young as eleven.

The Effects of Methamphetamine

Dr. Raymond Manning works with depressive disorders at Las Encinas Hospital, in Pasadena. He treats plenty of speed abusers, because "coming off the drug is so bad, and the depression it brings is so severe, that the user tends to do more [speed] rather than go through coming down again." Manning points out that meth tends to be highly addictive for two other reasons: It is very stimulating, and tolerance grows quickly, as does the user's intake.

"Amphetamine is a sympathomimetic drug," says Manning. "It mimics the effects of naturally occurring brain chemicals called catecholamines, which have a profound effect on our central nervous system." Like cocaine, amphetamine alters the brain receptors for dopamine, norepinephrine and serotonin—all of which affect our perception of pleasure.

While an extended state of euphoria is the intended goal, the side effects of prolonged use can range from mild panic to extreme paranoia accompanied by hallucinations. Jacob is currently treating a number of patients who, despite quitting speed some years ago, still experience aural and visual hallucinations. And addicts tend to be extremely violent.

Amphetamine was first synthesized in 1887 but didn't become popular until the pharmaceutical giant Smith Kline and French introduced it as Benzedrine, a nasal inhaler, in 1932. The Depression was in full swing, Prohibition was in effect, and the new drug was almost immediately abused by those looking for a new kick. Clever users soon discovered how to remove the inhaler's Benzedrine strip, which was then soaked in coffee—a picker-upper favored by the great jazz saxophonist Charlie "Bird" Parker. Methamphetamine, more potent than amphetamine and easy to make, originated in Japan in 1919. The crystalline powder is freely soluble in water, making it the perfect candidate for intra-venous use and abuse. Smoking the drug creates a rush almost as intense as in-jecting it, a fact that accounts (along with fear of needles) for the number of suburban kids lighting up. Still legally produced in the U.S. and most often pre-scribed for weight loss, meth is sold under the trade name Desoxyn.

Amphetamines tend to elevate mood, heighten endurance and eliminate fa-tigue—all of which explain the drug's popularity with the military. Methedrine, a brand of amphetamine in tablet form, was favored by German panzer troops, and according to medical records, Hitler was injected up to eight times a day with meth. Japanese factory workers, soldiers and pilots were given metham-phetamine. American Army Air Corps personnel stationed in Great Britain took good ol' Benzedrine—180 million pills. The practice continued through the Korean War and reached a fever pitch in Vietnam. Between 1966 and 1969, Americans ingested more government-issued speed in Vietnam than all British and American troops in World War II.

The Spread of Methamphetamine Use

Speed has been characterized as a trailer-park drug for decades. Traditionally, it was the drug of choice for long-distance truckers and college students pulling all-nighters. It has a high potential for abuse, however, and can, when misused over a long time, contribute to psychosis and violent behavior. "Look at some of the most violent crimes making the news," Heng says. "Like the Polly Klaas murder, where they found methamphetamine in the [accused killer's] trailer."

California is not the only state choking on an overabundance of speed. But the glut of product here has forced producers to seek new markets away from the West Coast. "Now, when we talk to other states," says Heng, "they're tying their labs and their big meth seizures back to people in California. And they're not too happy about that, ei-ther." The logic of this expansion is obvious, says Heng: "If you can sell it for twice as much in Florida, why

"Dr. Said Jacob has seen a marked increase in white, teen-age, male speed freaks."

not?" According to DEA statistics, only a few states have not reported a surge of this potent speed from California. "It's not something we're terribly proud of," says Heng.

Two other states are currently seeing a different kind of product: designer speed. In Hawaii, it's called ice, a superpure form of meth especially prepared for smoking. The effects of crystal meth, when smoked, can last well over four hours. Ice can keep the user high for up to twenty-four hours. In 1989, the media were buzzing with stories of an impending mainland U.S.A. invasion that would make the crack problem pale in comparison. Meth consumption in the continental U.S. may have increased in the interim, but ice has remained most popular in the Japanese, Filipino and Korean communities in Hawaii. Joe Parra of the DEA's Honolulu office thinks the reason is culturally related.

"It goes back to the '30s and '40s, when the use of amphetamine was pushed in Japan to enhance the industrial output of their society," Parra says. "And they trained the Koreans to manufacture amphetamine. That's remained an integral part of their society."

Other Designer Drugs

Meanwhile, in Michigan, a drug called cat (short for Methcathinone) has become a problem for users and police alike. "If you're smart enough to fog up a mirror, you're smart enough to make cat," says Jim McGivney, a public affairs officer with the DEA. Also called goob and morning star, cat is an extremely potent analog of amphetamine that can be whipped up from solvents purchased at a hardware store. For this same reason, the stuff is potentially lethal.

Cat seems to have been first produced in Michigan's Upper Peninsula, but it has spread throughout the state and into Wisconsin. Cat users are loyal to their low-rent drug. McGivney says: "Put a pound of coke and a pound of cat on a table and come back in an hour. The coke will still be there."

Talk to any law-enforcement official in just about any state and you'll hear that, yes, speed is indeed a problem to one degree or another. Yet, according to Heng, no one's listening. "If people really knew what was going on out there," she says, "they wouldn't stand for it, but the issue just isn't sexy at this point."

Alcohol Abuse Is a Serious Problem Among College Students

by Edward Malloy

About the author: *Edward Malloy is president of the University of Notre Dame in South Bend, Indiana, and chairman of the Commission on Substance Abuse at Colleges and Universities of the Center on Addiction and Substance Abuse (CASA) at Columbia University.*

Alcohol abuse on our nation's campuses is a crisis not just for our institutions of higher learning but for the entire nation as well. I speak from my experience both as chairman of the Center on Addiction and Substance Abuse College Commission and as president of the University of Notre Dame. The high prevalence of binge drinking on our campuses has devastating consequences. From violence to rape to the toll on academic performance and university life, the consequences of abusive drinking today are as apparent as they are deadly.

Statistics on Alcohol Abuse by Students

Most disturbing of the commission's findings is the increase in alcohol abuse by young women. Over the past fifteen years [between 1979 and 1994] the percentage of college women drinking with the intention of getting drunk has more than tripled, from approximately 10 percent to 35 percent.

The commission noted that alcohol abuse by both men and women on campus today has far more serious consequences for women than in the past:

—Ninety percent of all campus rapes occur when alcohol is being used by either the assailant, the victim, or both.

—Sixty percent of college women who have acquired sexually transmitted diseases, including AIDS, were under the influence of alcohol at the time they had intercourse.

—Ninety percent of violent crime and 53 percent of all injuries on campus

Edward Malloy, "Study of Alcohol Abuse on U.S. Campuses," *Origins*, June 23, 1994. Reprinted by permission of the author.

are alcohol-related.

—Alcohol is implicated in some 41 percent of all academic problems and 28 percent of all dropouts.

—Each year students spend more than $5.5 billion on alcoholic beverages—more than they spend on their books and on all other drinks combined.

—Two hundred forty thousand to 360,000 of the nation's 12 million current undergraduates ultimately will die from alcohol-related causes—more than the number who will get master's and doctorates combined.

To address this problem realistically requires an acknowledgment that the role of colleges and universities is not only to promote intellectual development, but also to nurture students' spiritual, social and emotional growth. Alcohol abuse must not be accepted as simply a part of the "rites of passage" of college students; it is destructive to students and the entire campus community. Collectively we must shift the culture away from alcohol.

The image of alcohol on campus must be changed. Rather than a liberating force that enables students to deal with academic and social stresses, it should be viewed as a crippling force that leads to academic and social failure, illness, violent behavior and even death.

Steps to Reduce Alcohol Abuse

The responsibility for addressing alcohol abuse is not solely that of the office of student affairs. It requires a strong commitment and increased activity on the part of each constituency in the campus community, from the board of trustees, administration and faculty to the student body, alumni and parents. Furthermore, this commitment must be reflected in a full range of prevention and treatment programs and in appropriate funding for these services.

Institutions of higher learning also must be willing to participate in and be judged by an "Alcohol Awareness Index" so that prospective students and parents can measure the degree to which each college and university is seriously addressing its alcohol problem. This index should be published in national college guides and should measure whether campuses ban all advertising and promotion of alcohol at social and athletic events and in campus newspapers; sponsor alcohol-free

"Most disturbing of the commission's findings is the increase in alcohol abuse by young women."

events where nonalcoholic beverages are available; serve beer, wine and other alcohol using trained servers only; promote positive and collective outlets that foster students' esteem; and provide a full range of prevention and treatment programs.

Federal and state governments can also take steps to assist schools in their efforts to change the campus culture. While considerable federal funds have gone into alcohol and drug prevention programs, evaluation of these efforts to determine what really works has been inadequate. Also typical two-year funding for these grants is not enough time to integrate programs into the campus community and determine whether or not they are effective. The Campus Security Act should be amended to require that crime reports identify the involvement of substance abuse. The reporting of these data must be carefully monitored to give the nation and individual colleges and universities a clear idea of the prevalence of alcohol abuse and the destructiveness of its consequences.

It is important to remember that alcohol abuse is not an insurmountable problem. Students are our hope; they are the future doctors, lawyers, artists, clergy, engineers and leaders of this nation. But we as college presidents, as trustees, as parents, as the citizenry must take the responsibility to assure that these students reach their potential. With a strong commitment of resources and the recognition that we are all responsible, we can combat alcohol abuse on campus and give students the education—academic, spiritual and social—that they deserve.

Substance Abuse Among Teenagers Is Not a Serious Problem

by Mike Males and Faye Docuyanan

About the authors: *Mike Males and Faye Docuyanan are graduate students at the University of California, Irvine. Males is the author of* The Scapegoat Generation: America's War on Adolescents.

On December 15, 1995, Health and Human Services Secretary Donna Shalala called her third major news conference in a year on teenagers and drug use. The tone was one of dire panic: "Your children are at risk," she declared. "We have a generation at risk."

Evidence of a Teen Drug Abuse Epidemic

Drug counselors, police and sheriff's deputies, and school officials throughout the United States have joined Shalala to proclaim a war on drugs in the schools—where they say kids are consuming drugs at younger and younger ages. Their typical estimates suggest that in any given Southern California high school, 50 to 80 percent of the students use marijuana, LSD, and/or crystal methamphetamine (speed). And many suggest that even cocaine, crack, and heroin are regularly consumed on school grounds.

But if literally hundreds of thousands of Los Angeles–area junior and senior high-school students take drugs on a regular basis at school, a major mystery is afoot: the case of the disappearing dope. Not only do the drugs fail to materialize in exhaustive undercover operations and searches, there is little evidence of any of the well-known consequences of drug abuse.

Toxicology reports of the Los Angeles County coroner reveal that in a metropolis of nine million, not a single teen, age thirteen through nineteen, died from a drug overdose during 1994. Of the 1,100 county deaths in 1994 considered drug-related—accidental overdoses, suicides, car wrecks, and other fatal

Mike Males and Faye Docuyanan, "The Return of Reefer Madness," *Progressive*, May 1996. Reprinted by permission from the *Progressive*, 409 E. Main St., Madison, WI 53703.

mishaps in which drugs were found—only six involved teens.

Nor do Los Angeles hospitals find a serious drug problem among youth. Teenagers made up only 3 percent of 36,000 emergency-room treatments during 1993 for drug-related injuries. The drug discovered in the systems of most adolescents receiving emergency-room treatment was aspirin or an aspirin substitute, which accounted for four times more teen emergencies than all street drugs combined.

In fact, the "teenage drug crisis" is a politically manufactured hoax. Take the Vernonia, Oregon, school district. It held itself up as a national symbol of teenage drug peril: "Students in a state of rebellion" due to "startling and progressive" drug abuse, its lawyer, Timothy Volpert, declared. But Volpert admitted that when the school tested 500 athletes during a four-year period at a cost of $15,000, it turned up just three "positives." Even so, Vernonia prevailed in the U.S. Supreme Court, which in 1995 upheld its effort to drug-test all student athletes.

Or take the Newport–Costa Mesa, California, school district, where officials also claimed extensive student drug activity. A series of unannounced sniff-searches by marijuana-trained sheriff's dogs throughout 1994 turned up zero evidence of drugs at the school. In a system with 7,700 junior and senior high-school students, dogs detected only ten lockers in which drugs might ever have been stored.

Targeting High-School Students

But mere facts have not slowed down the anti-teen-drug-use crusades. On December 7, 1995, just before Christmas vacation, fourteen-year-old Allison Smith (not her real name) was arrested at Redondo Union High School and charged with offering to sell marijuana to Los Angeles undercover sheriff's deputy Tim McCrillis, who had posed as a student. Smith was taken to the principal's office where investigators searched her for drugs. They found none. Then they handcuffed Smith to two other girls, and led her to a sheriff's van.

Outside the school, alerted reporters from major television and news-paper outlets had assembled, cameras and recorders whirring. School principal Robert Paulson and Redondo Beach police chief Mel Nichols had already set up a press conference. The next day, the local *Daily Breeze* banner-lined the arrest. The *Los Angeles Times* later ran a glowing story quoting only deputies.

"The 'teenage drug crisis' is a politically manufactured hoax."

Redondo Union High School's sprawling, park-like campus covers dozens of acres, commanding views of affluent oceanside houses and condominiums. Authorities singled the school out as a major center for student drug use. In a secret agreement with the school district, the Los Angeles County sheriff's department outfitted two young-looking undercover deputies as students in hallways and classes during fall term. After three months of daily full-time attendance and investigation at the 1,650-student school, police made seventeen arrests. Drug traffic at the school turned out to be "relatively light," deputies conceded. "I don't think it's an overwhelming problem," police chief Nichols admitted.

It was a problem for the arrested students. Upon recommendation of the Redondo/Manhattan school district, the school board summarily expelled all seventeen, including one special-education student, even though only two were found to have drugs in their possession.

> *"Mere facts have not slowed down the anti-teen-drug-use crusades."*

Most of the arrests turned out not to have involved actual exchanges of drugs, but only disputed claims of who approached whom and exactly what transpired. No witnesses have appeared to corroborate the deputies' versions of the disputed incidents.

The Disputed Incident

Smith's expulsion hearing was held before the Redondo/Manhattan school board on January 23, 1996. According to the transcript, Deputy McCrillis admitted the marijuana-sale charge against her was a "clerical error" and should have read (psilocybin) mushrooms. McCrillis stated he approached Smith "five or six" times during fall term and asked her to sell him drugs. He said that Smith, in an auto shop class on November 16, 1995, finally accepted $20 and agreed to sell him hallucinogenic "shrooms." Later she told him the money had been "ripped off" by the supposed supplier and never provided any drugs.

The deputy testified that other students witnessed the transaction. But he refused requests from Smith's attorney to name them. No one was called to support his version, and even he agreed that Smith never provided him with the drugs.

Smith categorically denied McCrillis's story. She testified that McCrillis approached her for drugs on a daily basis over a two-month period, entreaties which she refused. She said he finally placed $20 on a classroom table in front of her and left the room, and she was unable to find him to return the money. Further, Smith denied ever using drugs at school. After her arrest, she was tested for drugs. The test came out negative.

Smith had trouble explaining why she had not informed the principal that another "student" was persistently attempting to buy drugs from her, or why she did not turn over the $20 he paid her to school officials.

But McCrillis turned out to have a worse credibility problem. He claimed to have personally witnessed Smith "pull out a small baggie of mushrooms and ingest those" in a school classroom. Yet he did not report it to school authorities at the time, even anonymously.

When the testimony was completed, the entire case revolved around the $20 bill McCrillis said he gave to Smith under circumstances she disputed and to which no witnesses testified. Plenty of reason for a school board to give a ninth-grader the benefit of the doubt. But after the hearing, the board voted to expel Smith.

Another arrestee, eighteen-year-old Ryan Adcock, admitted that he did sell marijuana to McCrillis. Ryan, a special-education student, said McCrillis had approached him for weeks, "nearly every day, over and over again. He harassed students on a daily basis."

Ryan said he obtained some marijuana from an off-campus source and gave it to McCrillis. "It was my first time selling," he says. A couple of months later he was arrested. Another fifteen-year-old who had recently transferred to the school told the board, "I am not a drug dealer," but said he complied with the undercover agent's repeated drug requests in order "to make new friends in school."

> *"Youths have not played a serious part in the nation's drug-abuse problem for twenty years."*

Overzealous anti-drug warriors, or student junkies lying to save their hides? The media couldn't have cared less. *Los Angeles Times* reporter Eric Slater wrote a glowing news story praising a "well-managed narcotics operation"—a report cluttered with sarcasm about "hormone-addled sixteen-year-olds" and "later, dude" lingo. He based his story solely on the deputies' jocular anecdotes.

Three months after the arrests, parents say they know of only one student who has been criminally charged with selling drugs. Local police and the county sheriff's department, though eager to talk to the press at the time of the arrests in December, told us in March that they "didn't have time" to report how many students, if any, had been criminally charged.

Declining Teen Drug Abuse

Back in 1970, scores of L.A. teenagers died from drug overdoses. The city then accounted for one out of five teenage drug deaths in the United States. By the late 1970s, the L.A. teen drug carnage was over, and the city's youth drug toll has been very low ever since.

In June 1994, the federal Drug Abuse Warning Network (DAWN) released its annual survey of coroners in four dozen major cities. It found a record-high 8,500 deaths resulted from drug overdoses, drug suicides, and drug-related accidents in 1993. But teenagers made up just 2 percent of these deaths.

DAWN's companion survey of hospital emergency departments found that teens comprised just 3 percent of the 200,000 admissions involving heroin, cocaine, or marijuana. People under age twenty-one comprised only one in ten admissions to drug-abuse treatment programs in 1993, down sharply from one in six in 1987.

Teens aren't dying from drugs. They aren't going to hospitals or treatment centers for drugs. Schools that claim a big student drug scene can't produce evidence with dogs, undercover agents, random tests and surprise searches. Even among juvenile delinquents, the nation's highest-risk youth, a 1992 Bureau of Justice Statistics study found that young arrestees were the least likely of any age group to test positive for drugs.

In fact, three decades of drug-fatality statistics show that youths have not played a serious part in the nation's drug-abuse problem for twenty years. In Los Angeles County, teenage drug deaths declined by a staggering 90 percent from 1970 to 1994. Nationally, youth drug fatalities and injuries plummeted from 1970 to 1983 and have remained low ever since.

What, then, accounts for the incessant hype about a "teenage drug crisis" in news stories, documentaries, and official press releases since 1994?

What has become an annual media circus surrounding the release of the University of Michigan's "Monitoring the Future" survey of 50,000 junior and senior high-school students turns out to be governmental hyperventilation over increases in occasional use of marijuana. It's the return of Reefer Madness.

Media Hype over Statistics

The unreported findings of the Michigan survey were much less inflammatory than the headlines. Two in three high-school seniors, and seven in eight eighth-graders, had not smoked pot during the entire year preceding the survey. Only 2 percent of the seniors had used crystal methamphetamine, 4 percent had used cocaine, and fewer than 1 percent had used heroin during the previous twelve months And despite the usual press splashes over glue-sniffing, Wite-Out, and other supposed "new epidemics," surveys indicate that use of inhalants has been at fairly steady, low levels for the past two decades—2 to 3 percent of high-school seniors said they had used inhalants within the previous month, for example.

The usual orgy of political maneuvering followed the study's release. Shalala and White House drug-policy chief Lee Brown—who launched a personal "crusade" in 1995 to depict marijuana as an "addictive killer"—denounced proposed GOP cuts in the drug-war budget as "playing politics with the lives of America's children." Senate Judiciary Committee Chairman Orrin Hatch went one step further, announcing hearings on the Clinton Administration's "ineffectual leadership" on youth drug use. The Clinton Administration parried by calling a national conference of community leaders to discuss teenagers and drugs.

"The new Drug War of the 1990s increasingly busts casual drug use and drug possession."

For an Administration that initially promised to concentrate on treating hardcore addicts and targeting big-time drug sellers, the obsession (one Shalala in particular is in the grips of) now is to punish occasional, single-time marijuana use by primarily nonwhite teenagers. Whereas the Drug War of the mid-1980s focused on drug sellers and interdiction, the new Drug War of the 1990s increasingly busts casual drug use and drug possession. In 1994, three-fourths of the nation's record 1.4 million drug arrests were for simple possession, four in ten drug busts involved marijuana, and a record 312,000 were of teenagers—up 50 percent since 1990.

> *"While the teenage drug problem has diminished, the adult drug-fatality rate has been skyrocketing."*

Black youths have been particularly hard hit by the Clinton drug war. A black teenager is one-fifth as likely to die from drug abuse, but is ten times more likely to be arrested and dozens of times more likely to be imprisoned, than is a white middle-aged adult. A 1995 study by the Sentencing Project found that even though whites comprise the large majority of drug users, 90 percent of those imprisoned for drug possession were black or Latino. No change in policy is evident. Clinton's newly appointed drug czar, Barry McCaffrey, announced in March 1996 that he will target the bulk of the quarter billion dollars shifted to his office from the Pentagon budget at more law enforcement.

Clinton himself, illustrating what the *New York Times* called "another setpiece in his effort to showcase a 'values agenda,' " carried the anti-drug "personal statement" to a suburban Greenbelt, Maryland, high school in March 1996. Teenagers in the 1960s, he declared, "didn't really believe drugs were dangerous until it nearly destroyed a generation." But in nearby Baltimore, the coroner's report showed that while drug-abuse deaths had skyrocketed in the last four years, teenagers comprised none of the city's 458 drug-related deaths in 1994. Clinton is carrying his anti-drug message to the wrong audience: The worst drug abuse of his 1950s and 1960s generation is going on right now.

The Real Drug Crisis

There is indeed a large and growing drug-abuse crisis in the United States, also found most starkly in Los Angeles. It doesn't happen to be one health and drug officials want to elucidate, for obvious reasons: Its key elements are not pot, teens, and marijuana-leaf T-shirts, but hard drugs, middle-aged men, and Vietnam.

While the teenage drug problem has diminished, the adult drug-fatality rate has been skyrocketing. In 1994, 554 Los Angeles adults died of drug overdoses and an equal number were the victims of drug-related suicides and accidents. The new drug crisis couldn't be more inconvenient for drug-war officials. Not only is it erupting among the wrong age groups and for the wrong reasons, its timing is terrible.

What occurred during the decade-long period when drug overdoses were doubling and drug-related murders quadrupling? The multi-hundred-billion-dollar

War on Drugs was inaugurated in 1983, escalated in 1986, and justified throughout with official promises that the crusade was vital to a reduction in drug abuse and crime.

Nationwide, in 1983, 2,700 Americans died from drug overdoses, a number that had been declining for the previous decade. In 1994, that number nearly tripled to 8,000.

In 1983, about 500 Americans died in murders attributed by the FBI to narcotics. In 1994, 1,800.

Since 1983, the rate of drug-abuse deaths among American adults has risen 120 percent. Exploding rates have occurred not among teens but among middle-aged men nationwide.

In 1980, about 400 American men, age thirty-five to fifty-four, died from drug overdoses. In 1994, a projected 3,500 to 4,000. Drug-related suicides doubled. The big killers: heroin, cocaine, pharmaceutical drugs, and alcohol mixed with drugs.

Drug death rates are now so high among middle-aged men that they dwarf all other classes. Middle-agers are now twenty times more likely to die from drugs than are teenagers, and middle-agers account for half of all drug deaths. Hospital statistics show that death is just the tip of an iceberg of drug abuse in this age group.

Causes of Middle-Age Drug Abuse

What could be causing this huge surplus of middle-aged drug abuse?

A big part of the answer may be Vietnam. An ongoing project of the Centers for Disease Control, one not publicly advertised during the drug hoopla of the last seven years [between 1989 and 1996], was to monitor mortality among returning Vietnam veterans. The results of this study were grim. The project found greatly elevated rates of suicide, homicide, and fatal accidents among Vietnam veterans for the first five years after their return, statistics that hold true for previous wars as well.

Most of the heightened death toll apart from drug-related deaths subsided by the late 1970s. But researchers reported that drug-related deaths were proving a major exception. The level of drug-abuse fatality

> *"Exploding rates [of drug-abuse deaths] have occurred not among teens but among middle-aged men nationwide."*

among Vietnam veterans was much higher than that of the rest of the population and had continued to rise through 1988, the date of the latest report.

But the government doesn't want to face up to the drug legacy of the Vietnam War. It would rather concoct a crisis around a 3-percentage-point increase in self-reported, occasional marijuana smoking by high-school students. And it has downplayed studies by the psychology departments at the University of California at Los Angeles and at Berkeley that suggest that moderate pot smoking has no long-term effects and does not correlate with personality problems in teenagers.

A further, tragic irony is that growing drug abuse among middle-aged Americans has real-life impacts on the very youths federal policymakers say they are concerned about. A 1992 Boston juvenile-court study found that of 200 children and youths removed from their homes after suffering severe physical and sexual abuse, two-thirds had parents who abused drugs or alcohol. Our own interviews with teenage mothers and alternative high-school students turned up incident after incident of drug-addicted parents, household violence, children and teenagers forced to stay home from school to take care of younger siblings, and parents so debilitated by drugs that they could not care for their families.

The War on Teens

Clearly, an undercover operation like the one at Redondo Union High School could be inflicted on any group in society. Given plenty of money, sufficient time, and aggressive sting operations, any institution—high schools, universities, Congress, the White House staff, the *Los Angeles Times*, police and sheriff's agencies—could be relentlessly targeted, and a few arrests would result. But why target teens? They are not the ones who use drugs the most, yet today's anti-drug warriors aim to inflict harsher punishments on adolescents than on groups that display more serious drug problems.

Today, Allison Smith's only contact with school has been one hour per week, during which she picks up her independent-study assignments and returns home to complete them. She admits enjoying the arrangement a bit—studying in front of the TV, on her own time, no hassle.

She's puzzled at the logic, though.

"If I was truly a drug dealer, I'd have a lot of time to deal now," she joked. "I would have thought they'd want to keep us in school."

Teenage Use of LSD Is Not a Serious Problem

by Jacob Sullum

About the author: *Jacob Sullum is a senior editor of* Reason, *a monthly libertarian magazine.*

In June 1993 Ann Landers ran a letter from a reader who had recently seen an article "about how LSD is making a big comeback among the youth of America"—the kind of story that has appeared in newspapers and magazines with some regularity during the past few years. "I was a teenager in the 1960s," he wrote, "and although I was never involved in the drug scene, I remember hearing a lot of horror stories about young people jumping in front of trains, off roofs, and out of windows while under the influence of LSD. I am very concerned for this new generation of LSD users." The reader urged Landers to publish accounts by former acid users of "how this drug ruined their youth and possibly their adult years as well," along with letters from people who had "lost loved ones because of LSD."

Alarmism About LSD

Landers agreed there was cause for alarm. "The prospect of this dangerous drug making a comeback is bone-chilling," she replied. "This mind-altering drug has been responsible for many deaths. Flashbacks, which can occur years after the user has sworn off the drug, can be frightening."

This exchange illustrates how the conventional wisdom about LSD is propagated: People who don't know what they're talking about pass on hearsay and misinformation, blithely reinforcing each other's ignorance. As Leigh A. Henderson, an epidemiologist, and William J. Glass, a drug-abuse treatment specialist, note in their introduction to *LSD: Still with Us After All These Years*, this ignorance is all the more remarkable given half a century of experience with the drug, including more than a decade of legal use in psychotherapy, hundreds of clinical studies, and recreational use by millions of Americans since the early 1960s. This fascinating book summarizes that history and describes the findings of research on the current LSD scene sponsored by the National Institute on Drug Abuse. Ann Landers ought to read it.

If she did, she would learn that the "big comeback" of LSD looks more like a blip. "After the intense interest and experimentation it generated in the late 1960s and early 1970s," Henderson writes, "LSD use has settled into an entrenched pattern among a limited population. . . . The level of LSD use has varied little between the late 1970s and early 1990s." Past-month use of LSD by high-school seniors, for example, has been around 2 percent since 1975. (In the general population, the corresponding figure is less than 0.3 percent.)

The Truth About LSD's Dangers

Landers might also reconsider her assertion that LSD "has been responsible for many deaths." In general, Henderson writes, "LSD appears to pose few if any risks to physical health. . . . Severe adverse reactions to LSD are rare, and death due to an overdose of LSD is essentially unknown." Fears that the drug might cause brain damage, genetic abnormalities, or insanity have not been substantiated. And while LSD can impair judgment, thereby contributing to accidents, so can other, more popular drugs, including alcohol.

As for the LSD flashback, it can probably best be understood as a sudden, vivid recollection of a dramatic, emotional experience—a phenomenon that is not limited to drug users. Contrary to popular belief, flashbacks are not caused by brain damage or LSD residue, and they are generally quite brief. *Pace* Ann Landers, Henderson reports that flashbacks "seldom occur more than a few months after the original trip." Furthermore, "a large proportion of those experiencing flashbacks (35 to 57 percent) have reported finding them pleasant (a 'free trip')." It's hard to imagine Landers noting that "flashbacks can be enjoyable."

Which is precisely the point. Even when anti-LSD propagandists are not spouting nonsense, they talk only about the drug's potential drawbacks, creating the impression that LSD generally leads to bad trips, horrible accidents, and scary flashbacks. Clearly, this cannot be true. If it were, personal observation and word of mouth would long since have eliminated LSD use, and the drug warriors would have nothing to worry about. So LSD begins with an obvious yet frequently overlooked point: Taking LSD is *fun*. True, it's a kind of fun that many people (not just Ann Landers) do not understand, which is one reason LSD use remains concentrated among a small percentage of

> *"LSD use remains concentrated among a small percentage of middle-class white males in their late teens and early twenties."*

middle-class white males in their late teens and early twenties. But by and large, the pleasure that people get from LSD is worth the cost involved.

The initial cost is quite low, especially compared to other drugs. A dose sufficient to produce a trip of five to seven hours can be had for a few dollars. But despite the low price, there is little risk of compulsive use. You have to set aside a significant block of time for each trip, and tolerance develops quickly (if you take the drug every day, it stops having the desired effect). Which is not to say that people never take LSD more often than is prudent. The book describes users who became obsessed with the drug, spending most of their time tripping or recovering from trips. But this pattern is rare. Indeed, most people who try LSD use it only a few times.

Good Trips and Bad Trips

Although LSD is a very powerful substance—less than 100 micrograms is enough for a trip—the user's state of mind and environment can have a decisive impact on the drug experience. Bad trips generally result from taking the drug in the wrong mood, the wrong setting, or the wrong company. In Chapter 1 [of *LSD*], "What Is a Trip—And Why Take One?," anthropologists James Mac-Donald and Michael Agar describe several bad trips, all of which were characterized by a loss of control caused by unexpected developments (an argument, the arrival of police). Experienced users learn to drop acid with friends in secure, predictable situations. MacDonald and Agar speculate that this requirement may help explain why LSD is not popular in the inner city. A threatening, chaotic environment is not conducive to a good trip.

"By and large, the pleasure that people get from LSD is worth the cost involved."

"The irony," note MacDonald and Agar, "is that one objective of a trip is to lose control, but loss of control is the cause of a bad trip." LSD users seek a *controlled* loss of control, an experience something like a roller-coaster ride, where there is a predictable beginning and end, where the sense of danger is part of the thrill but the true risk is minimal. The best cure for a bad trip is the simple reassurance that the experience will pass.

Why Teenagers Might Use LSD

As Henderson notes, the term *hallucinogen* is something of a misnomer, since neither LSD nor the other drugs classified under that label produce true hallucinations. The user is aware that the distortions and illusions triggered by LSD are not real. In this respect, an LSD trip is analogous to a lucid dream.

On the other hand, dream images are generally more vivid and complete than LSD images. In this sense, what you see on an acid trip pales in comparison with what you see every night when you go to sleep. And LSD trips are tied to reality in a way that dreams are not. The wall is not really undulating, but the wall is there; the light is not really dancing, but the light is there. LSD lets the user see familiar things in a new and interesting way. It's not hard to understand why this would appeal to a bored teenager.

And it's not hard to understand why it would frighten people like Ann Landers. Dreams, after all, are restricted to sleep. Even if they can be more convincing and dramatic than an acid trip, they do not reach out and grab reality. Still, in trying to fathom the LSD experience, it's worth reflecting on the fact that dreams, for all their irrationality and frivolity, appear to be indispensable. Subjects deprived of REM sleep (the phase in which dreams occur) start to get loopy pretty quickly. To keep our sanity, it seems, we need to lose our minds now and then.

Alcohol Abuse Is Not a Serious Problem Among College Students

by Kathy McNamara-Meis

About the author: *Kathy McNamara-Meis is a senior editor of* Forbes Media-Critic.

Not only did the announcement confirm the worst about today's college students, but it demanded action. According to a study by the Center on Addiction and Substance Abuse at Columbia University (CASA), released on June 7, 1994, by CASA chairman Joseph A. Califano, Jr., "binge" drinking has dramatically increased on America's campuses, leading to a rise in its "disastrous consequences . . . including death, violence, rape, and the spread of sexually transmitted diseases, such as AIDS."

Media Hype on College Drinking

Such a disturbing message, coming from Columbia University and announced by no less than Joe Califano, a Washington superlawyer who served in the Lyndon Johnson White House and as Secretary of Health, Education and Welfare for President Jimmy Carter, made big news. On June 8, the *Washington Post* and *USA Today* ran front-page stories, and dozens of newspapers across the country picked up wire service reports. The CASA study also was reported in *Insight* and *U.S. News & World Report*. The *New York Times*'s Anna Quindlen excerpted parts of the study in an op-ed column headlined, "The Legal Drug." And syndicated columnist Suzanne Fields, concerned about the apparent increase in heavy drinking among female college students, commented that "feminism doesn't require men and women to be equally stupid."

The story also attracted the interest of television. On NBC's *Today*, Stone Phillips asked Califano: "I can think back to college days when going out and having drinks on Friday night was fun, it was a pressure release, maybe, from the academic, you know, issues, but are kids just not getting the message that this can be dangerous, especially this kind of binge drinking?"

Califano responded, "I think what's happening, Stone, is that the consequences . . . are much more serious. . . . Today you go out, and a woman gets raped, somebody gets beat up. We have examples of murder on campus." Califano made similar remarks in other television appearances.

Questions About Drinking Statistics

Through various media, CASA succeeded fabulously in getting out the statistical particulars of its message: (1) "60 percent of college women who have acquired sexually transmitted diseases, including AIDS and genital herpes, were under the influence of alcohol at the time they had intercourse"; (2) "90 percent of all reported campus rapes occur when alcohol is being used by either the assailant or the victim"; (3) "The number of women who reported drinking to get drunk more than tripled between 1977 and 1993"; and (4) "95 percent of violent crime on campus is alcohol-related."

Remarkable numbers. But are they valid?

"The percentage of heavy drinkers on campus has remained constant for decades. About 43 percent of college students report binge drinking each year."

"If I were teaching a research class, I would use this CASA report as an example of what not to do," says Professor David Hanson of the State University of New York at Potsdam, who has studied alcohol use on campus for over twenty years among more than 30,000 students. Citing voluminous published evidence contradicting CASA's findings, Hanson scolds the commission for what he describes as its haphazard research and reliance on unscientific evidence.

Dwight Heath, a professor of anthropology at Brown University and one of the world's leading scholars on alcohol use among various cultures, says CASA's statistics on alcohol-related violence are "absurd." Heath's decades of research have persuaded him there is no such correlation.

Hanson, Heath, and other students of alcohol use . . . are in agreement that the percentage of heavy drinkers on campus has remained constant for decades. About 43 percent of college students report binge drinking each year.

These researchers could have been reached easily enough on the day Califano released the CASA study. It is astonishing that no reporter appears to have made such calls. As it happens, many of the statistics heralded as "news" by CASA are more than five years old. Other simply are not credible.

Alcohol and AIDS

For example, the finding that 60 percent of college women who have contracted sexually transmitted diseases such as AIDS were under the influence of alcohol at the time of infection appears to have been pulled from thin air. The source for this figure, as cited in the CASA study, is the Advocacy Institute's publication *Tackling Alcohol Problems on Campus: Tools for Media Advocacy.* That publication cites as its source a June 1990 University of California at Berkeley publication titled *Consider the Connections: Alcohol/drugs, Sexuality/sociability and Beyond.* But this number wasn't the result of original research, or even fact-checking by its author, Cathy Kodama, a health educator at Berkeley. Kodama told me she got the statistic from a speech she

> *"Is it really true that 90 percent of all campus rapes occur when alcohol is being used?"*

had heard given by the director of student health services at the University of Wisconsin. *Consider the Connections*, she says, was only a student handout that was "not intended to reflect any kind of original research." In other words, she cannot vouch for the accuracy of her own number. She adds, "I'm a little concerned at how far this has been taken."

The CASA report suggests that a frightening explosion of AIDS on college campuses has been caused in part by alcohol use. Interestingly, Kodama's handout does not mention any specific connection between AIDS and alcohol. In a move perhaps designed to attract media attention, CASA simply inserted the phrase "such as AIDS" after the words "60 percent of college women who have acquired sexually transmitted diseases." But deep inside the CASA report it was also noted that only 3,000 students nationwide have tested positive for HIV, the virus that causes AIDS. This, out of a college population of 12 million. The percentage of HIV-positive students thus works out to .025. This very low figure is no reason for college administrators to dismiss the threat of AIDS, but it does put in another light what CASA presents as a horror.

Alcohol and Rape

Moving to another CASA number, is it really true that 90 percent of all campus rapes occur when alcohol is being used? This statistic does not appear to exist in the published research available on rape. According to Elizabeth Board of the Distilled Spirits Council of America (DISCA), a trade association whose members obviously benefit from the $3.17 billion college market for alcoholic beverages, this number has a strange origin. DISCA's own interest duly noted, I discovered Board is right.

Noticing that the CASA study did not provide a footnote indicating the source for this figure, Board called CASA's vice president and director of policy and research, Jeffrey Merrill, who told her it came from an April 1992 document called the *"Put on the Brakes" Bulletin*, which is published by the Department of Health and Human Services' Office for Substance Abuse Prevention (OSAP). When contacted, Merrill said he remembered that someone had questioned this number, and that he couldn't remember its source.

Why was that? The 90 percent figure does appear in the *Bulletin* and the document does indicate a source for the statistic—a story published on September 20, 1991, in the *Maine Campus*, a student newspaper at the University of Maine. "Link Between Alcohol and Rape Shown in Lecture" reported on a talk by the university's director of substance abuse services. According to the story, the speaker cited a *Ms.* magazine study as the source of his statement that use of alcohol is involved in 90 percent of campus rapes.

> *"Wechsler and Isaac found virtually no change in the proportion of frequent heavy drinkers among college women."*

But the lecturer misspoke or else was misquoted by the student reporter because the *Ms.* study, actually funded by the National Institute for Mental Health in cooperation with the Ms. Foundation, offers no such number. It's not surprising that in my interview with CASA's Merrill he couldn't remember the source for it. There is none.

More Accurate Figures

The *Ms.* study's findings on this point were that 74 percent of men who claimed to have raped said they were drinking or using drugs at the time of the assault and that 75 percent of these men perceived that their victims were using intoxicants as well. The study states that 55 percent of the female victims reported consuming alcohol or taking drugs at the time of the rape, and 73 percent of these women believed their assailants were under the influence of drugs or alcohol. These more complex and thus less dramatic data were mentioned in, but not touted by, the CASA report. Not surprisingly, these data were ignored by most media, which reported the incorrect, but often-highlighted, 90 percent figure instead.

Notably during the *Today* interview with Califano, Stone Phillips confronted another guest, Dr. Cheryl Presley of Southern Illinois University, with the 90 percent figure. Presley, who oversees one of the most widely cited studies of college drinking responded: "Our institute has not pulled in that particular statistic. However, we are verifying and supporting that information because we found that over 25 percent of the college students who report binge drinking, both male and female, are saying they've been victims of sexual assault and have either been victims or have been perpetrators." This was a bizarre statement for one of the nation's preeminent alcohol researchers to make, yet Phillips did not ask the obvious follow-up question of how she could accept such divergent numbers.

Drinking Among College Women

As for CASA's figure of a 300 percent increase in the number of college women drinking to get drunk, the parents of college women everywhere will be glad to learn that the statistic is also dubious. The survey that produced it was limited to drinking at a handful of colleges in Massachusetts in the years 1977 and 1989, hardly a national sampling.

Conducted by Henry Wechsler and Nancy Isaac of the Harvard School of Public Health, the survey compared apples and oranges—drinking by college students of all ages ('77) to that by freshmen only ('89). The authors of the CASA study surely must be aware of the problem with this kind of comparison, for as they observe, "freshmen are more likely to drink, drink more, and drink more often than seniors" and "consumption of alcohol declines each year a student is in school." Though Wechsler and Isaac do not believe freshmen drink more than older students, their imbalanced comparison raises questions about their findings.

> *"The idea that 95 percent of violent crime on campus is alcohol-related should be viewed with skepticism."*

More importantly, CASA distorted Wechsler and Isaac's findings by excerpting dramatic, negative developments with regard to alcohol consumption while ignoring positive ones. For instance, the CASA study failed to mention that Wechsler and Isaac found virtually no change in the proportion of frequent heavy drinkers among college women and, in fact, had found an 11 percent increase in the proportion of female collegiates abstaining from alcohol.

Finally, the idea that 95 percent of violent crime on campus is alcohol-related should be viewed with skepticism. According to CASA, the source of this figure is the Student Right-to-Know and Campus Security Act, which requires universities receiving government funds to provide information regarding the graduation rates of student-athletes. But consider the text of the statute: "Approximately 95 percent of the campus crimes that are violent are alcohol- *or drug-related*, [but] there are currently no comprehensive data on campus crimes." (Emphasis added.) There are many numbers that, added together, equal 95. The CASA study asks the public to believe that the authors of the statute added 0 and 95, with 95 being the percentage for alcohol-related violent crimes. But as the text of the statue indicates, its authors could not have done any such thing, because of the lack of "comprehensive data."

Questioning the Study's Purpose

CASA's Merrill makes no apologies for the study's methodology or its numbers, maintaining that the latter are taken from respectable journals or documents. "That's about all you can ask for out of a study like this." He adds, "You obviously tracked these statistics back further than we did."

Told about flaws in CASA's data, Monte Lorell, front page editor of *USA Today*, says his paper wouldn't have run the story had the editors been aware of them. "No one likes to get burned like this," he says. One reason his paper trusted CASA as a source, he adds, was Califano's involvement.

It may be argued that the unskeptical journalism on the CASA study was harmless, since CASA's goals appear to be virtuous. The study recommends working to "shift the college culture away from accepting alcohol abuse and its consequences as part of the 'rites of passage,'" and trying to "control the abuse of alcohol at on-campus functions." It advises the federal government to "evaluate alcohol and drug programs paid for by the Fund to Improve Post-secondary Education and disseminate information on what works and what does not to all colleges and universities," and to "fund more research on a spectrum of prevention and treatment interventions that match the needs of different groups on campus." What could possibly be the harm in CASA's approach and the media's uncritical acceptance of it when the commission's recommendations are so worthy?

Researchers in the field of alcohol consumption say there is something harmful about the study's message. Michael Haines, who researches drinking at Northern Illinois University, says that distortions of what is really happening on campus have the effect of "normalizing the misbehavior we're trying to prevent." Since 1990 he has been studying the "misperceptions of social norms." This theory holds that if students perceive something to be the norm, they tend to alter their behavior to fit that norm, even if it isn't reality. If, however, they are presented with the actual norm, they will conform to it. So if students think heavy drinking is normal, they'll drink more. If they think responsible drinking is normal, they'll drink more responsibly.

An Alternative to Reduce Drinking

Haines says his research shows that the majority of students are responsible drinkers. As a result of these findings, he headed a campaign to educate students and free them from the burden of trying to conform to a negative and invalid stereotype. His university's approach, which involves distribution of fliers, ads in the student newspaper, and incentives for students who internalize the message that heavy drinking is not the norm, has achieved a nearly 23.7 percent reduction in heavy drinking. This is an impressive decline considering that the nationwide percentage of college students who drink heavily has remained stubbornly constant for decades.

Opening a line of inquiry yet to be explored by the media, Haines sees misrepresentations such as those found in the CASA report as a way "to keep the public, who can pressure lawmakers, believing that the problem [of alcohol abuse] is real and big and should be supported and funded. It's a way for organizations to lobby for funding and expand their power base. It is one of the uglier phenomena of our times."

Chapter 3

How Can Teenage Addiction Be Prevented?

CURRENT CONTROVERSIES

Preventing Teenage Addiction: An Overview

by Sarah Glazer

About the author: *Sarah Glazer is a freelance writer in Washington, D.C.*

Parents of children who attend a respected private school in Washington, D.C., met in 1995 to discuss ways to keep their kids from using drugs. They had good reason to meet. Half the students on the senior class ski trip, the parents had just learned, smoked marijuana on the outing.

Drug-Generation Parents and Their Children

One mother expressed a worry echoed by several of the baby-boomer parents at the meeting. "How do I talk to my seventh-grader about not using drugs," she asked, "when it was our generation that ushered in the drug revolution in the 1960s?"

Mothers and fathers around the nation are facing the same dilemma, whether their children attend public or private schools. Most parents don't want their teens using drugs. But many adults experimented with drugs in their youth, and most went on to drug-free, successful lives. What should they be telling young people about drugs? And what message should schools and government anti-drug agencies be delivering?

"Parents are scared to talk about it with their kids," says Alyse Lynn Booth, communications director at the Center on Addiction and Substance Abuse (CASA) at Columbia University in New York City.

In July 1995, CASA, which is headed by former Health, Education and Welfare Secretary Joseph A. Califano Jr., released a national survey showing that teens consider drugs the biggest problem for people their age. Yet fewer than half the parents surveyed have had serious discussions with their children about the implications of drug use, the survey found.

"Baby-boomer parents are uncomfortable talking about drugs," Booth says. In focus groups conducted in conjunction with CASA's survey, "Some parents

Sarah Glazer, "Preventing Teen Drug Use," *CQ Researcher*, July 28, 1995. Reprinted with permission.

said they would lie to their kids if asked if they ever used drugs," she adds.

The company that conducted the survey for CASA interviewed 2,000 adults and 400 adolescents ages twelve to seventeen. Of the tenth-graders surveyed, more than half said that they had been offered drugs to buy or share and that they had friends who had used marijuana. (The survey did not ask the young people if they used drugs themselves.)

"Kids really see drugs as a problem, and parents and schools are letting them down," Booth says. "Kids [in the survey] were talking about the fact that drugs are all over the place," but the problem "is being pretty much ignored [by adults]. Drugs went off the radar screen in the 1990s."

Increased Teenage Drug Use in the 90s

The problem takes on added significance because, after more than a decade of declining drug use among high school students, the latest national surveys show continued increases in illicit drug use, particularly among the youngest teens.

From 1991 to 1994, the proportion of eighth-graders who say they used marijuana in the previous year doubled to 13 percent, according to University of Michigan social scientists who have been tracking national trends since 1975. From 1992 to 94, marijuana use among tenth-graders increased 66 percent while use among twelfth-graders increased 40 percent. In 1994, 25 percent of the tenth-graders and 31 percent of the seniors surveyed said they had used marijuana in the past year.

While marijuana has had the most dramatic turnaround in the 1990s, the survey found that the use of other drugs has been rising gradually as well. These include LSD and other hallucinogens, stimulants, barbiturates and, in 1994, cocaine and crack.

At every grade level from eighth through twelfth, about one in five or six students has tried sniffing an inhalant—mainly common household substances such as glues, paint thinner and aerosols. Such substances produce instant highs but can cause brain damage or death. The use is greatest among eighth-graders, experts say, probably because inhalants are so easy for them to get. In fact, eighth-graders are more likely to have used inhalants than any other drug, except alcohol or tobacco. Twenty percent admit to ever using an inhalant. However, an even larger proportion (26 percent) admit to having been drunk at least once, and 46 percent say they have smoked cigarettes.

> *"Many adults experimented with drugs in their youth, and most went on to drug-free, successful lives."*

Lloyd D. Johnston, the lead investigator of the Michigan survey, notes that overall drug use among high school students is still far below its peak in the late 1970s and early '80s. More than 60 percent of high school seniors surveyed from 1977 to 1985 admitted to trying an illicit drug. But starting in the early 1980s, drug use began to decline and in 1994 stood at 46 percent of seniors. Marijuana use declined even more dramatically, from a peak of 60 percent of twelfth-graders in 1980 who said they had ever tried it to only 38 percent in 1994.

Nevertheless, Johnston says he finds the recent increases in use, though modest, "reminiscent of the drug epidemic 30 years ago in that some of the same drugs that started that epidemic—marijuana, LSD, amphetamines—are now on the rise."

Johnston credits the nationwide anti-drug campaign launched in the 1980s, targeting young people through school programs and the media, for driving down drug use. Even

> *"Johnston credits the nationwide anti-drug ["Just Say No"] campaign launched in the 1980s . . . for driving down drug use."*

though the "Just Say No" message conceived by first lady Nancy Reagan was often ridiculed as overly simplistic, "It was during that time that there emerged a single message for young people," Johnston says. "It was loud, and it was repeated. That [kind of effort] has declined considerably.". . .

The new trend in drug use poses a dilemma for drug educators and policymakers: Should government and schools beef up efforts to warn kids of the dangers of drugs, or will warnings have a boomerang effect, lowering adults' credibility and actually prompting more youngsters to try drugs? Some psychologists argue that experimentation with drugs, including alcohol, is a normal part of adolescent development in American society today.

But others see more of a problem. "I think it's gone beyond experimentation," says Barbara C. Thornton, principal of Largo [Florida] High School, recently recognized by President Bill Clinton for getting students with drug problems into treatment programs. "I think it's become a part of what young people do," she says, noting that drug abuse in many cases replaces the more innocent Saturday night diversions of generations past, such as bowling or skating. . . .

Drug Abuse Resistance Education (DARE)

By law, every K–12 school in the country receiving federal money must have a drug prevention program starting in kindergarten. But these programs vary widely, from one-shot assemblies to multi-week courses.

"The Department of Education spends several hundred million dollars a year in the nation's schools on substance-abuse prevention programs," says Larry Seitz, director of research on school-based programs for the National Institute on Drug Abuse (NIDA). "But they don't know if that makes kids less interested in using drugs or more interested."

In fact, the single most popular school program nationwide has little influence on children's use of tobacco, alcohol or marijuana, according to a 1994 study commissioned by the Justice Department's National Institute of Justice (NIJ). Known as DARE (Drug Abuse Resistance Education), the program is carried in all fifty states and in over half the nation's school districts. It uses specially trained uniformed police officers to teach schoolchildren, mainly fifth- and sixth-graders, how to say no to drugs.

In rural Davie County, North Carolina, for example, the seventeen-session DARE program culminates in an end-of-year assembly at which children, to the applause of parents and local politicians, read their essays making a commitment not to take drugs.

But the NIJ-funded study concluded that the program was less effective in changing fifth- and sixth- graders' drug-taking behavior than so-called "interactive" drug-prevention pro-

> *"The single most popular school program nationwide has little influence on children's use of tobacco, alcohol or marijuana."*

grams. Such programs rely heavily on students' participation in role-playing and discussions to give them a more accurate sense of what their peers think of drugs.

The All-Stars program, for example, recently had seventh-graders at the Lexington [North Carolina] Middle School debating the question, "Would you use marijuana because a friend of yours uses it?" Students in the program had to stand next to a sign that represented their viewpoint.

"It reinforces the kids that have made a commitment to lead a drug-free life," says teacher Becky Pace. Indeed, she points out, "They get torn down so much by other kids for being against drugs" that they are often surprised to find three-fourths of their class standing with them against drug use.

Health education teacher Gary Hankins, who hosted the All-Stars program at the school, says, "I had DARE in my classroom for the last four years, and I like this better. What's so neat about it is the students do the actual teaching, but they don't realize it."

By contrast, "Many DARE lessons are didactic question-answer sessions between police officer and students rather than interactions between students," says Susan T. Ennett, an author of the federally funded evaluation of DARE programs. "DARE is a popular program, but in terms of how we spend our government dollars it seems appropriate to look at the effectiveness as well as how well-liked it is—and the results are disappointing."

Controversy over Drug Education Evaluations

The study raised a storm of controversy when it was completed in 1994, angering DARE officials and local supporters with its negative conclusions. The two-page summary of the study issued by the sponsoring NIJ emphasized the researchers' positive conclusions about its popularity among teachers, parents and school staff but gave short shrift to the researchers' negative findings on DARE's minimal impact on drug use. The findings on drug behavior, the summary said, "should be interpreted cautiously because of the small number of studies used for analysis and the low level of drug use among fifth- and sixth-graders."

"The evaluation was done on our previous curriculum," says William F. Alden, deputy director of DARE. "We're less didactic now than we were in the early '80s, when an officer would stand up and lecture to the kids."

But social psychologist William B. Hansen, who has been studying drug-prevention programs for twenty years, expresses skepticism. "They don't have any evidence to back that up—that it works."

One of the main problems with DARE, he says, is that its timing is off. "Fifth-graders love you," he says. "They're bouncy and cuddly. They're not suspicious when you walk in with a uniform." By junior high, the same children are searching for independence from adults and concerned above all about social acceptance by their peers, he says. "Once they get into that society, everything you've taught them in fifth grade is out the window."

Davie County's experience is instructive. Students who received DARE training in the fifth grade actually increased their tobacco use between seventh and ninth grades (from 13 percent of the students in the program to 37 percent, according to student surveys in 1991 and 1993). "When they went to seventh grade, we began to see some of the motivation with the DARE program was beginning to wear off, and they were being influenced by their peers, says Betty B. Griffith, the county's director of school health services. The survey prompted administrators to add a two-week booster session in seventh grade.

Despite the disappointing statistics, School Superintendent William Steed says DARE is so popular that, "If we said we were going to drop it, our citizens would not allow us to do that."

"We've seen a tremendous difference, not necessarily in statistics going down, but in students acting in a positive way toward law enforcement," explains Griffith. "We think this is a positive aspect of the program in addition to just talking about substance abuse.". . .

> *"School Superintendent William Steed says DARE is so popular that, 'If we said we were going to drop it, our citizens would not allow us to do that.'"*

Confronted with criticisms of DARE and other popular school drug programs, federal drug official Fred W. Garcia responds that schools cannot, by themselves, change society's behavior. Garcia, deputy director for demand reduction in the White House Office of National Drug Control Policy, compares the drug situation with the public health campaign to reduce cavities. That effort included a major environmental change—putting fluoride into the water.

Yet when it comes to drugs, he argues, "We have an environment that markets drugs as something to make yourself feel better chemically"—from alcohol to Tylenol. "I don't think anyone can say prevention does or doesn't work. We haven't tried the full system.". . .

Legalization and Other Education Approaches

As national surveys show, close to half of America's teenagers will try an illicit drug (not including alcohol) by the time they reach twelfth grade. Yet this important fact is papered over by most drug education programs, critics who favor drug legalization say.

The no-use approach taken by most prevention programs "can have a backlash effect, attracting teenagers' curiosity to a forbidden fruit," says Rob Stewart, spokesman for the Drug Policy Foundation, which favors considering legalization. "You have to be honest. You have to say there are good things [about drugs]. People do find that they can use drugs for different reasons—whether for inspiration or relaxation or recreation. But until you're of age, that's out of your purview. No program says that, as you can imagine."

"Drug prevention programs as taught in the United States are a disgrace," says John P. Morgan, a professor of pharmacology at the City University of New York Medical School. "They are overwhelmingly influenced by the abstinence model, which says the only way to deal with dangerous substances, particularly marijuana, is to abstain."

Morgan, who favors legalization, advocates what he calls the harm-reduction approach. If he had his druthers, Morgan says, he would tell a classroom that he knows some percentage of them will take marijuana and ecstasy. Consequently, he would provide tips on how to reduce the potential dangers under the influence of drugs.

In the case of marijuana, his advice would include designating a non-smoker to drive marijuana users

> *"The no-use approach taken by most prevention programs 'can have a backlash effect, attracting teenagers' curiosity to a forbidden fruit.'"*

home from a pot party, using a water pipe to help filter out particles harmful to the lungs and taking only one or two "hits," or puffs, if the joint (cigarette) contains potent marijuana.

In the case of ecstasy, he would tell students, "You have to be careful about sexual expression because your judgment is changed. Everyone feels wonderful and happy—hugging and bodies are wonderful—so people forget the rules about sexuality."

To Jonathan Shedler, a professor of psychology at Adelphi University in Garden City, New York, drug-prevention programs are barking up the wrong tree by failing to distinguish between teenage drug experimentation and drug abuse. While it's true that peer pressure often accompanies teen drug use, he says, only a minority of those users will go on to abuse drugs. "Experimentation in this culture is the norm in terms of what most adolescents are doing," he says. "We're devoting a lot of resources to discouraging experimentation without any meaningful impact on drug abuse."

Chapter 3

Gateway Drugs

Most people who use marijuana do not go on to use hard drugs, national surveys show. But most drug addicts started by using marijuana and other milder substances like alcohol and tobacco.

In a report issued in 1994, the Center on Addiction and Substance Abuse endorsed the view that marijuana, alcohol and tobacco are "gateway" drugs. Use of those substances, especially early in life, increases the probability that a person will go on to hard drugs, the report concluded.

The report, which is based on a review of other studies, concluded that children twelve to seventeen years of age who use marijuana are 85 times more likely to use cocaine than children who never used it. Furthermore, the report said that the younger children are when they use marijuana, the more likely they are to use cocaine, heroin, hallucinogens and other illicit drugs. While only 20 percent of individuals who smoke pot after age seventeen use cocaine, 60 percent of children who smoke pot before age fifteen move on to cocaine, the report stated.

> *"Use of [marijuana, alcohol, and tobacco], especially early in life, increases the probability that a person will go on to hard drugs."*

"[T]he message is clear," the report concluded. "It is imperative to step up health promotion and disease prevention programs to encourage children not to smoke, drink or use marijuana."

The link between cigarette smoking and later marijuana smoking among teens gained prominence following press reports on the National Conference on Marijuana Use, held July 19–20, 1995, in Arlington, Virginia. It was noted at the conference, which was sponsored by the National Institute on Drug Abuse, that teen cigarette smoking, like marijuana use, has risen after several years without change.

Smoking among eighth-graders surged 30 percent from 1991 to 1994, according to the University of Michigan's annual "Monitoring the Future" survey. Almost 19 percent of eighth-graders surveyed in 1994 said they had smoked in the previous thirty days, compared with 14.3 percent in 1991. Study director Johnston noted that tobacco use among teens has been correlated with marijuana use. Various surveys have shown teen tobacco use to be correlated with delinquency, early intercourse without contraceptives and drinking. Previous Michigan surveys have found that high school seniors who smoke are more likely to use illegal drugs.

Experimentation vs. Drug Abuse

Some experts and activists in the field have blasted the CASA report for claiming, without hard evidence, that soft drug use leads to hard drugs.

"Unlike many other studies," says Shedler, "the CASA study has not been published in a peer-reviewed scientific journal. Its conclusions are scientifically unfounded."

Morgan at the City University of New York notes that a large majority (about 80 percent) of high school seniors who smoke marijuana never use other drugs. Therefore, he says, it would be more appropriate to dub pot a "terminal" rather than a "gateway" drug.

Indeed, another review of the literature published in 1994 by the congressional Office of Technology Assessment (OTA) also advanced a cautious explanation of the progression from alcohol, tobacco and marijuana to other illicit drugs. "Because many individuals who use substances do not go on to substance abuse, and because use at one level does not guarantee use at a higher level, these stages are descriptive, but not predictive," the study concluded.

Shedler is among several psychologists who view heavy drug use as merely a symptom of longstanding psychological problems, not the result of early drug taking. In a twenty-year study of 101 children in the San Francisco Bay area, beginning when they were in nursery school, he found that the majority had tried marijuana at least once by age eighteen, but only 21 percent had become heavy users and had tried at least one hard drug.

"The question is not who experimented and who didn't, because virtually everyone did," says Shedler. "The question is why for the majority of adolescents some experimentation is just that—experimentation—and they grow up to be productive citizens, but for a small minority drug experimentation leads to drug abuse."

Parents Must Decide How to Talk to Children About Drug Use

by John Leland

About the author: *John Leland is a senior writer at* Newsweek.

Like a lot of people her age Elizabeth Russell, forty-two, figures she got into drugs when the getting was good. She was young, she was curious and the hippies still wore flowers in their hair. When grown-ups tried to caution her about the dangers of drugs, she remembers, "I thought it was a joke—reefer madness. We laughed our heads off about it. We knew different."

Concerns of Parents

These days, as the mother of a thirteen-year-old son, Russell no longer finds the cautionary huffing so funny. A self-employed businesswoman in the San Francisco Bay Area, she avoids even the occasional puff of pot. "Now I just eat," she laughs. And though she looks back on her experiments as mostly harmless and often fun, she doesn't want her son Jett to follow her example. To that end, she says, she has been open with him about her past, admitting that she had tried not just marijuana but also cocaine and LSD. So far, Jett is a hard-core basketball jock, and strongly anti-drug. If he did start smoking pot, Russell says, "it would concern me a little bit; I don't know what I'd say." She swears she would not react like her own mother. "My mom came down so hard I went harder on it."

Russell's dilemma is one of the thornier challenges now facing the baby boom. Having celebrated drug use as a rite of adolescent passage, the Woodstock generation now has children of its own, either slogging through or approaching their teen years. And some of the parents are getting pretty, uh, *uptight* about it. In a survey of parents with teenage kids, 75 percent said they "would be upset if my child even tried marijuana," and 77 percent said "parents should forbid their kids to use drugs at any time." For a generation that believes it skewered anti-drug hypocrisy, this can be a source of real parental anxiety. How much should you tell your kids about your own past? When? How can you just say no, when you spent your salad days just saying yes? In short, how does the drug generation now talk to its children about drugs?

One answer is: not very effectively. After a decade-long decline, rates of teenage drug use have risen sharply since 1992, in some cases nearly doubling. More than 41 percent of 1995 high-school seniors had tried marijuana or hashish, the highest rate since 1989. Nearly 12 percent had tried LSD. Though usage rates are still well below their peak of the late '70s, kids seem to be experimenting earlier. More than one in five eighth graders said they used an illicit drug in the last year. And experts warn that some marijuana available today is much more powerful—up to thirty times stronger—than it was in the past. At the same time, the percentage of kids who say their parents have talked to them about drugs has dropped. Says Alan Leshner, director of the National Institute on Drug Abuse, "Many parents are . . . afraid that their kids will say, 'Didn't you try it then?'"

Talking to Kids About Drug Use

Elizabeth Crown, forty-five, found herself in this position with her daughter Emily, nine. Crown smoked marijuana with her friends in the late '60s, and says now that she doesn't "feel totally negative about the experience. Whether right or wrong, it brought friends together. We had fun." When Emily asked her whether she had smoked pot, she said yes. "She asked me what it did," says Crown. "I said it makes me stupid. I told her there's really nothing worse than feeling like you're not in control." She says she doesn't feel hypocritical about telling Emily to do as she says, not as she did. "I knew people who escalated and became addicts later, and therefore I feel that I can say, 'It really isn't a smart thing to do'."

Drug counselors are divided about how much you should tell your kids about your own experiences. Leshner advises parents to shift the conversation away from themselves, especially for those who enjoyed the ride. "You have to turn it around from 'I did it and I lived, so therefore you can do it and live' to 'My friend Sally didn't live'." Also, he says, we know more now about the harmful effects of marijuana.

> *"In short, how does the drug generation now talk to its children about drugs?"*

Child psychologist James Garbarino, director of the family-life development center at Cornell University, argues that parents should avoid telling their children too much about their own drug use, just as they wouldn't share the details of their sex lives. "They're in a role of authority. In general they should be cautious." Young children especially can be confused by parents' simplistic confessions that they used drugs. "They'll overgeneralize," says Garbarino. "They'll see something on TV about crack addicts. They'll think, 'My parents are criminals, they're going to go to jail, I'm going to be left behind'."

Sarah Wenk, thirty-eight, a computer consultant in Woodstock, N.Y., has cobbled together a compromise for discussing her past experiences with her son Conor, six. She'll tell him the broad story now, the fine points when he gets older. Though she thinks that some drugs, used in moderation, are basically benign—

> *"For many parents, the worst scenario isn't for their kids to try drugs . . . but for them to be secretive about it."*

"I'm in favor of pleasurable indulgences"—she also thinks her son is too young to understand the distinction. "He's so little now. Last night I asked him what he knew about drugs. He said, 'You can't take drugs, they're really really bad for you.' I said why? He said he didn't know." For now, this is exactly where she wants him. "Then as he gets older, I can be less black and white. If I say drugs are bad but some aren't as bad, he's too young to make some of those decisions."

The drug question can get dicier for parents who still smoke pot. A documentary filmmaker from New York, who spoke only anonymously, still likes to get high occasionally and views his drug experiences, apart from cocaine, as largely beneficial. He hasn't raised the subject of drugs with his kids, ages eight and eleven, because he hasn't needed to. "They're ahead of me," he says. "The propaganda at school is so strong that they bring the subject up. They say drugs are terrible, anybody who does them is stupid. I nod my head and say nothing, figuring in due time they will experiment." He makes no moral distinction between marijuana and alcohol. But though he drinks in front of his two children, he wouldn't think of lighting up. "One's legal," he says. "One isn't."

For Sarah Wenk, as for many parents, the worst scenario isn't for their kids to try drugs—they concede that they might—but for them to be secretive about it. In this, parents' experience can be a blessing. "If Conor is going to try things," says Wenk, "I hope he'll keep me posted." The call for candor cuts both ways. Jett Russell, the basketball jock, is glad his mother told him about her past. "I think I probably would have figured it out," he says. "I'm glad she quit when she did."

But for all the candor and sensitivity, what many parents really want is what their parents wanted: that their kids never mess with any drug, any time. In an online discussion group for parents, which she hosts, Wenk recently arrived at what she thought was an appropriate age for Conor to experiment with drugs: forty.

Society Should Educate Teenagers About Alcohol's Dangers

by Antonia C. Novello

About the author: *Antonia C. Novello is a former surgeon general of the United States.*

When I began as Surgeon General in 1989, I decided to take on illegal underage drinking because it was about kids, it was about prevention, and back then, I thought it was a fairly contained, "doable" effort.

The Public Health Campaign Against Underage Drinking

Little did I realize that the avalanche of public concern and public health data I found made this issue—alcohol—possibly one of the most significant public health challenges we face today in our country.

I have spent much of my time speaking out on this problem. I have gone to small towns, I have spoken to advocacy groups, I have held press conferences and issued an eye-opening series of reports on underage drinking.

I have done everything I can think of to wake Americans up to the real health risks and potential tragedies of saying "well, at least my kid doesn't do drugs—he only drinks beer." This American complacency is killing our youth: *I tell you, it is time we all wake up to the fact that alcohol is a drug—one of the most powerful drugs we have.*

Since I began my efforts, I have learned a great deal—but most importantly, I learned that this country is in need of "Alcohol Education 101"—from the communities to the Congress.

I've also become convinced that parents and communities play a key role in prevention—a role that can't be played right unless it is shared and supported by our schools, our policymakers, our health care providers, our law enforce-

From Antonia C. Novello, "Alcohol and Tobacco Advertising: Prevention Indeed Works," speech delivered at the Center for Substance Abuse Prevention, Washington, D.C., February 8, 1993.

ment officials—and, most importantly, by media and advertising.

We know that preventing illegal underage drinking works best when the message is straightforward and clear—not mixed. When the messages our children get at home are the same ones they get at school, and are reinforced by the community, their peers, and the media.

The more I get involved in this issue, the more finger-pointing I see. The alcohol industry would have us believe that kids and their families are responsible for underage drinking problems. The kids would have us believe that it is their friends, and the merchants, and all of us "apathetic" adults who are the problem.

The advertising industry would have us believe that we public health "nuts" are the problem—after all, the industry is only working to create "brand loyalty," not to increase market share by luring our youth.

I tell you, the time has come to move past all the finger-pointing—and work together, with one voice, to solve this complex problem. We can't just point a finger at parents, and their kids, as industry would have us believe, just as we can't simply point a finger at the industry alone, as many advocacy groups would have us believe.

The Community's Role in Preventing Teenage Drinking

The key to our prevention efforts is the role of the community in helping us solve the problem of illegal underage drinking and other drug abuse.

Each of us, in our multiple roles as parents, school and community leaders, health care providers, national figures, holds a key to helping our sons and daughters through this thorny aspect of growing up.

Each of us shares the responsibility for becoming part of the solution, rather than a large part of the problem.

Let me take a few moments to share with you some of the findings we have made on illegal underage drinking based on the data we have collected to date:

> *"Parents and communities play a key role in prevention."*

Since September 1990, I have conducted a carefully thought-out campaign against illegal underage drinking—a campaign that culminated in the invaluable series of eight reports done for me by former Health and Human Services (HHS) Inspector General Richard Kusserow. And a campaign that prompted the Department of Education to publish a compilation of these reports into a booklet called, *Youth and Alcohol: Select Reports to the Surgeon General.*

From those eight reports, I learned a lot.

• I learned that 10.6 million, or half, of our young people in the seventh through twelfth grades drink, and that nearly a half million binge on a weekly basis—five drinks, one after another.

In fact, in 1992, Dr. Lloyd Johnston reported that 1 in every 8 eighth graders—or 13 percent—reported recent binge drinking—and 1 in 4 eighth graders—or 25 percent —are current drinkers (drinking at least once in the month prior to the survey).

• The reports also showed me that youth drink to handle stress and boredom, and they drink to change their mood. They don't just drink at parties or with their friends—they drink alone. This is worrisome, because for so long we were told that adolescents drink because of peer pressure.

The Reasons Children Drink

• The reports showed me that adolescents really don't know what they're drinking: 2 out of 3 adolescents could not identify whether a product contained alcohol simply by the shape of the bottle (e.g., wine coolers) or the information on the label.

• In addition, nearly 80 percent of our youth do not know the difference between the amount of alcohol in whiskey and beer.

• And the labels do not help. Based on a 1935 law, unless States require it, the alcohol content of beer and malt liquor are not listed on the labels of these beverages. The idea, back then, was that identifying the alcohol content would entice people to drink. To this I say that the consumer of 1935 is not the consumer of today! We must look into these outdated laws in the context of today's knowledgeable consumers.

• I also learned that our young people today can simply walk into a store and buy alcohol without needing an I.D. In fact, they consume 35 percent of all wine coolers sold and 1.1 billion cans of beer a year in this country.

> *"Adolescents really don't know what they're drinking."*

• What's more worrisome—I discovered that enforcement of underage drinking laws by states and localities is uneven at best, its enforcement non-existent at worst, and riddled with loopholes, in most cases.

• Witness the fact that:

• In 5 states and the District of Columbia, it's not specifically illegal for minors to purchase alcohol;

• In 38 states it's not specifically illegal for minors to possess alcohol because of exceptions to the law;

• In 21 states it's not specifically illegal for minors to consume alcohol; and

• In 44 states minors can sell and serve alcohol without adult supervision.

In November 1991, I released a report on alcohol advertising because I strongly believe that the widespread nature of alcohol advertising evokes glamorous, pleasurable images that can mislead youth about alcohol. Images and messages that directly contradict our promotion of healthier lifestyles and risk avoidance.

Based on the facts, we have found that the use of alcohol by young people can lead to serious health consequences far beyond those well-known figures about drinking and driving: I am talking about crime, serious injury, date rape, vandalism, theft, truancy, absenteeism, and school dropouts. These are the tragic, yet seldom-discussed consequences that few people ascribe to alcohol use.

The Influence of Alcohol Advertising

But our facts, our warnings, and our health promotion messages are entirely at odds with the enticing drum beat of alcohol beverage ads that say, "Drink me and you will be carefree. Drink me and you will be cool. Drink me and you will have fun! Drink me, and there will be no consequences."

Let me be very clear here. The kinds of ads that appeal to our young people are—to some degree—appealing to all of us. But our young people, in their search for identity, their doubts about their own popularity and sexual attractiveness, are particularly vulnerable to the lure of tantalizing promises—however false.

My report on alcohol advertising found that youth are especially attracted to four different types of ads—those which make lifestyle appeals, make sexual appeals, use sports figures or youth heroes, or show people engaged in risky activities.

We need to address each of these enticement strategies, but above all, we need to look into ads that show risky activities, the ones in which the consequences of performing such activities while drinking are dangerous and not depicted. (E.g., whether it is the skier coming down the slope, ready for a beer, or the swimmer, the surfer, or the boater.)

> *"Our facts, our warnings, and our health promotion messages are entirely at odds with the enticing drum beat of alcohol beverage ads."*

We have data that are *unequivocal* in their conclusions—alcohol and recreational activities are a dangerous mix. Accordingly, we must speak out against the involvement or depiction of alcohol use in activities where physical and mental coordination is critical.

The Dangers of Alcohol Use

After all, we know that it takes a 150-pound man one to two hours to metabolize the alcohol in one beer alone. Our kids need to hear this, and they need to understand it.

In addition, two studies on adolescent drowning found that from 40 to 50 percent of young males who drown used alcohol prior to their deaths, and 69 percent of boating accidents are secondary to alcohol intake. And yet we continue to see alcohol ads showing poolside and beach parties where young people gather.

Since the report on advertising was issued, I have called for industry's voluntary elimination of alcohol advertising that appeals to youth on the basis of lifestyle appeals, sexual appeal, and sports heroes, and particularly the ones showing risky activities—as well as advertising with the more blatant youth appeals of cartoon characters.

And I have said to the industry that if industry has developed voluntary codes, then by God, they should be the first ones to adhere to them.

Clearly, this has not been enough. *The time has come for the public to become the pulpit.*

As opinion leaders, as educators, as parents, as those entrusted with the future of our youth, the time has

> **"Industry should be made more accountable, and parents should be more demanding that the industry protect their children."**

come for us to ensure that the true consequences of the misuse of alcohol and other drugs by our youth are widely known throughout the land and throughout learning institutions of this country, through the media, and through the halls of Congress.

We must convince the skeptical and the uninformed among us—and in particular, the industry—that illegal underage drinking is not an acceptable rite of passage—it is a passage to tragedy that all of us must address.

Industry should be made more accountable, and parents should be more demanding that the industry protect their children, in turn.

Knowledge is power, and the time has come to use this power to protect our children.

The final set of reports done for me by the Inspector General documented the "unrecognized consequences" of alcohol that rarely capture headlines. They highlighted what the misuse of alcohol by our young people can mean to them. My friends, as you well know, there is much more to alcohol than dying—much more to alcohol than cirrhosis of the liver.

Alcohol's Links to Adolescent Problems

There is *living* proof of this.

• Alcohol has been linked to involvement with crime—both in perpetrators and victims, involvement in risky sexual activities, and in increasing the risk for all sorts of injuries.

• In addition, alcohol has been linked to poor school performance, involvement in vandalism, theft, and truancy, and the added pain of suicide.

• We also learned that those who have been drinking are almost twice as likely to be injured than those who have not been drinking at all.

• We learned that approximately one-third of our young people who commit serious crimes have consumed alcohol just prior to the commission of the crime, and one-half of college students who were crime victims admitted to being under the influence of alcohol and/or drugs at the time of the crime, as well.

• And we also learned that alcohol misuse was involved in the vast majority of sexual assaults and risky sexual behavior going on on our campuses.

As we continue to see more and more adolescents infected with HIV—and as heterosexual transmission gains in prominence among adolescent girls as well as boys—we will have an overwhelming health crisis to contend with, if we do not pay attention now to the issues of alcohol, youth, drugs, infallibility, and risk-taking.

My friends, there is a complete lack of public awareness about the potential link between alcohol use and its undue consequences.

Witness the fact that only 5 percent of adolescents who have drinking problems are diagnosed and referred by their doctors! The greatest number come from the social services or from the courts.

Let's stop kidding ourselves and stop the denials—our kids are drinking—and we are condoning it! We cannot remain as bystanders and watch an entire generation falter.

In the presence of all these data, we must continue to teach our children, as we also press for responsible industry action and realistic, enforceable regulations.

Parents Should Teach Teenagers to Drink Responsibly

by Elizabeth M. Whelan

About the author: *Elizabeth M. Whelan is president of the American Council on Science and Health, a consumer education organization that studies health and nutrition.*

My Colleagues at the Harvard School of Public Health, where I studied preventive medicine, deserve high praise for their 1995 study on teenage drinking. What they found in their survey of college students was that they drink "early and . . . often," frequently to the point of getting ill.

Professional and Personal Concerns

As a public-health scientist with a daughter, Christine, heading to college this fall, I have professional and personal concerns about teen binge drinking. It is imperative that we explore *why* so many young people abuse alcohol. From my own study of the effects of alcohol restrictions and my observations of Christine and her friends' predicament about drinking, I believe that today's laws are unrealistic. Prohibiting the sale of liquor to responsible young adults creates an atmosphere where binge drinking and alcohol abuse have become a problem. American teens, unlike their European peers, don't learn how to drink gradually, safely and in moderation.

Alcohol is widely accepted and enjoyed in our culture. Studies show that moderate drinking can be good for you. But we legally proscribe alcohol until the age of twenty-one (why not thirty or forty-five?). Christine and her classmates can drive cars, fly planes, marry, vote, pay taxes, take out loans and risk their lives as members of the U.S. armed forces. But laws in all fifty states say that no alcoholic beverages may be sold to anyone until that magic twenty-first birthday. We didn't always have a national "21" rule. When I was in college, in the mid-'60s, the drinking age varied from state to state. This posed its own risks, with underage students crossing state lines to get a legal drink.

In parts of the Western world, moderate drinking by teenagers and even children under their parents' supervision is a given. Though the per capita consumption of alcohol in France, Spain and Portugal is higher than in the United States, the rate of alcoholism and alcohol abuse is lower. A glass of wine at dinner is normal practice. Kids learn to regard moderate drinking as an enjoyable family activity rather than as something they have to sneak away to do. Banning drinking by young people makes it a badge of adulthood—a tantalizing forbidden fruit.

Christine and her teenage friends like to go out with a group to a club, comedy show or sports bar to watch the game. But teens today have to go on the sly with fake IDs and the fear of getting caught. Otherwise, they're denied admittance to most places and left to hang out on the street. That's hardly a safer alternative. Christine and her classmates now find themselves in a legal no man's land. At eighteen, they're considered adults. Yet when they want to enjoy a drink like other adults, they are, as they put it "disenfranchised."

Comparing my daughter's dilemma with my own as an "underage" college student, I see a difference—and one that I think has exacerbated the current dilemma. Today's teens are far more sophisticated than we were. They're treated less like children and have more responsibilities than we did. This makes the twenty-one restriction seem anachronistic.

Teaching Responsible Drinking in the Home

For the past few years, my husband and I have been preparing Christine for college life and the inevitable partying—read keg of beer—that goes with it. Last year, a young friend with no drinking experience was violently ill for days after he was introduced to "clear liquids in small glasses" during freshman orientation. We want our daughter to learn how to drink sensibly and avoid this pitfall. Starting at the age of fourteen, we invited her to join us for a glass of champagne with dinner. She'd tried it once before, thought it was "yucky" and declined. A year later, she enjoyed sampling wine at family meals.

"American teens . . . don't learn how to drink gradually, safely and in moderation."

When, at sixteen, she asked for a Mudslide (a bottled chocolate-milk-and-rum concoction), we used the opportunity to discuss it with her. We explained the alcohol content, told her the alcohol level is lower when the drink is blended with ice and compared it with a glass of wine. Since the drink of choice on campus is beer, we contrasted its potency with wine and hard liquor and stressed the importance of not drinking on an empty stomach.

Our purpose was to encourage her to know the alcohol content of what she is served. We want her to experience the effects of liquor in her own home not on the highway and not for the first time during a college orientation week with free-flowing suds. Although Christine doesn't drive yet, we regularly reinforce the concept of choosing a designated driver. Happily, that already seems a widely accepted practice among our daughter's friends who drink.

Averting Tragedies

We recently visited the Ivy League school Christine will attend in the fall. While we were there, we read a story in the college paper about a student who was nearly electrocuted when, in a drunken state, he climbed on top of a moving train at a railroad station near the campus. The student survived, but three of his limbs were later amputated. This incident reminded me of a tragic death on another campus. An intoxicated student maneuvered himself into a chimney. He was found three days later when frat brothers tried to light a fire in the fireplace. By then he was dead.

These tragedies are just two examples of our failure to teach young people how to use alcohol prudently. If eighteen-year-olds don't have legal access to even a beer at a public place, they have no experience handling liquor on their own. They feel "liberated" when they arrive on campus. With no parents to stop them, they have a "let's make up for lost time" attitude. The result: binge drinking.

We should make access to alcohol legal at eighteen. At the same time, we should come down much harder on alcohol abusers and drunk drivers of all ages. We should intensify our efforts at alcohol education for adolescents. We want them to understand that it is perfectly OK not to drink. But if they do, alcohol should be consumed in moderation.

After all, we choose to teach our children about safe sex, including the benefits of teen abstinence. Why, then, can't we—schools and parents alike—teach them about safe drinking?

Casual Drug Use Must Be Fought Vigorously

by Lee P. Brown

About the author: *Lee P. Brown is the former director of the Office of National Drug Control Policy. He is now a professor of sociology at Rice University in Houston, Texas.*

Editor's note: This speech was delivered to the American Cities Against Drugs Conference held in Atlanta, Georgia, in May 1995.

I am inspired by this show of unity. It comes at a most critical juncture in the ongoing debate about the direction of drug policy in this country. Our coming together sends a visible, forceful message to the nation that we mean business—that we are at one purpose in our opposition to drug legalization.

A United Effort Against Drug Legalization

When you sign the Atlanta Resolution this afternoon, you will have committed your cities to a most significant proposition. That proposition says that we will fight drug use and addiction with all our might, that we will not fall prey to frustration. We will not throw up our hands in surrender. Your presence here demonstrates that you are not about to give up on your cities, on your citizens, and most of all on your children.

Our discussions during this meeting are evidence to all who would listen that we are not going to be distracted by silly arguments about why drugs should be legalized. There is no need to debate the facts. The facts are well-known, and we have no intention of seeing these facts manipulated and twisted into a mistaken conclusion.

When I was asked to address you today on the topic "Why the United States Will Never Legalize Drugs," I welcomed the opportunity to make clear my position and the position of President Bill Clinton on this issue. The President and I are vehemently opposed to legalization in any form. Legalization is not an idea whose time has come. It is nothing more than a surrender to the forces that would poison our children and our communities.

From Lee P. Brown, "Why the United States Will Never Legalize Drugs: Protecting Our Children," speech delivered at the American Cities Against Drugs conference, Atlanta, Ga., May 15, 1995.

I have seen the current debate taking form over the last few months. I have heard the crescendo of voices raising the legalization issue to national debate, doing all that they can to make this an issue of legitimate discourse. The debate is not new; it all started many years ago with a few voices that were easy to dismiss. But recently, we have had even more national pundits and media giants jumping on the bandwagon, waving the banners of legalization.

I am sure many of you saw the television program, "The War on Drugs: Searching for Solutions," the ABC special that aired in April 1995. I was shocked that here was a major television network masquerading before the public what was little more than a "Rah-Rah" legalization message. It purported to tell the whole story about drugs, but instead only emphasized those points that made legalization sound reasonable and rational. And, of course, we know that legalization is neither a reasonable nor rational policy for this country.

A Mixed Message for Young People

One of the things that bothers me most about the legalization argument is the mixed message it sends to our young people. The legalization gurus shamelessly advance a laissez-faire attitude about drugs, at a time when we need to be unequivocal with our youngsters that drugs should never be a choice for them.

Any reputable study you want to look at will document that drug use among the young is on the rise. Youngsters are taking chances with drugs because many perceive that the risks are lessening, that the social strictures against drug use are becoming less rigid. So while we need to make clear in no uncertain terms that drug use is not acceptable at any level, we have so-called responsible adults trumpeting a wishy-washy defeatist attitude to impressionable adolescents.

What is particularly dismaying is that much of the legalization debate is based on the faulty notion that since people are going to use drugs anyway, we might as well get out of the way and let them. The truth, however, is so often obscured that many do not know that we have had some significant success in reducing the rate of casual drug use.

Over twenty years ago, estimates of drug use among Americans went as high as 24 million, but we now estimate that the number of Americans who use illegal drugs is down to some 11 million. That's a reduction of more than half. And a recent study done by my office shows that Americans are spending less on illegal drugs, not more. In 1993, Americans spent $49 billion on illegal drugs, down from $64 billion in 1988.

> *"We need to be unequivocal with our youngsters that drugs should never be a choice for them."*

In addition, the FBI will announce shortly that in 1994 the crimes of murder, rape, robbery, burglary, theft, auto theft, and aggravated assault declined substantially in a majority of large American cities. I believe that this decline can be attributed to two things in particular. One is an increase in community policing efforts that put more officers on the street; and the second reason is that more and more communities are taking an aggressive posture against crime. It is this same kind of aggressive stance that we must take against the spread of drugs.

So it is clear that we have made some progress. Why on earth would we want to reverse this trend by making drugs legal and available to anyone who wanted to use them?

Violence Is Associated with Drug Use

Without laws that make drug use illegal, some experts estimate that we could easily have three times as many Americans using cocaine and crack. This has a direct correlation to the crime and violence that grips so many of our neighborhoods and communities. The proponents of legalization would have us believe that crime would go down if drug use was legal, but an honest look at the facts belie this argument.

Statistics tell us that almost half of those arrested for committing a crime test positive for the use of drugs at the time of their arrest. Making drugs more readily available could only propel more individuals into a life of

> *"Many do not know that we have had some significant success in reducing the rate of casual drug use."*

crime and violence. Contrary to what the legalization proponents say, profit is not the only reason for the high rates of crime and violence that are associated with the drug trade. Research has shown that drug users who are severely addicted are responsible for the commission of many crimes. The legalization proponents fail to recognize or choose to ignore the fact that drugs are illegal because they are harmful—to both body and mind.

When we look at the plight of many of our youth today, especially African American males, I do not think it is an exaggeration to say that legalizing drugs would be the moral equivalent of genocide. Making addictive, mind altering drugs legal is an invitation to disaster for our communities that are already under siege. How could we as a nation even consider the possibility of helping more human beings destroy themselves—not to mention what they do to their families and neighborhoods? As leaders and policymakers, we have a solemn obligation to our citizens to propose and enact policies for the common good.

The Clinton Administration has heard the American people's concerns about crime and violence. We have no intention of considering any proposals, no matter how they are dressed up, that would serve to heighten Americans' fears about their personal safety and security.

The Strategy to Fight Drugs

Let me warn you, however, that the legalization proponents do have an advantage over those of us who are committed to staying the course. They can wave their banners and proselytize to their heart's content, without any concern for real policy creation. They can simply be against something without ever coming up with a coherent strategy to change the drug problem as we know it today. As Director of the Office of National Drug Control Policy, I have no such luxury. I have a commitment to the American people to be for something, and let me outline briefly just what we in the Clinton Administration are for.

We have a National Drug Control Strategy that is both comprehensive and balanced. We are going to marshal all of the resources at our disposal to educate young people about the dangers of drug use.

> *"Making drugs more readily available could only propel more individuals into a life of crime and violence."*

We are going to work tirelessly to break the cycle of crime and violence that so often accompanies the drug trade. We will do this by providing treatment to hardcore drug users who cause a disproportionate share of the violence that grips our cities.

And we intend to punish those who insist on breaking the law. This is why the Anti-Violent Crime Control Act is so important to the nation. It will put more police officers on the street to make neighborhoods safer for the residents who live there, and it will also provide critical prevention programs to help our young people stay off of drugs and out of trouble.

As one who has served in law enforcement for over thirty years, there is one thing that I am sure of and that is the impossibility of solely arresting our way to a solution to crime and drugs. We definitely need strong law enforcement measures, but that alone is not the answer.

A recent poll of police chiefs and county sheriffs across the nation found that 42 percent want more drug and alcohol prevention programs. They cited neighborhood watch programs, community policing, and anti-gang programs as critical to effective law enforcement efforts.

We believe in these same kinds of programs, because we know they work. Giving more drugs to people won't help anything. Providing treatment, however, to those who need it will make a big difference.

Creating an environment where open air drug markets can flourish won't make anyone feel safer. But having police officers trained in the methods of community policing can go a long way toward making communities the havens they were intended to be.

Protecting Children

Sending a message to children that the nation will turn its head while they experiment with drugs that can devastate them mentally and physically is morally reprehensible. Yet guiding them and providing them with prevention and education programs before they even consider the possibility of drugs will make them much stronger and wiser for the effort.

We have always been a nation that protects its children. Why would we change that now to accommodate a frustrated few who want to let drug abuse run amok through our society?

Why would we advance any proposition like the legalization of drugs that would undermine our national resolve to revitalize our communities? Why would we sanction any policy that would threaten the well-being of our youngest and most vulnerable citizens? I have no doubt that we are wasting time with arguments about the legalization of illegal drugs. This is time that could be better spent discussing responsible directions for this nation. . . .

Our message continues to be—help those who need help. Arrest those who sell drugs. But never, ever surrender. The future or our nation depends on it.

Drug Abuse Resistance Education Works

by Bureau of Justice Assistance

About the author: *The Bureau of Justice Assistance, a bureau of the U.S. Department of Justice, provides technical assistance and administers federal grants to state and local government programs for the prevention of drug abuse and violent crime.*

Drug Abuse Resistance Education (D.A.R.E.) is a validated, copyrighted, comprehensive drug and violence prevention education program for children in kindergarten through twelfth grade. D.A.R.E. represents a collaborative effort between school and law enforcement personnel. The program is nationally coordinated by D.A.R.E. America, with input received from State and local agencies and communities.

What Is D.A.R.E.?

The D.A.R.E. curriculum is designed to equip elementary, middle, and high school students with the appropriate skills to resist substance abuse, violence, and gangs. More than 22,000 community-oriented law enforcement officers from 7,000 communities throughout the country have taught the core curriculum to more than 25 million elementary school students. In 1995 alone, it is expected that 5.5 million children representing 250,000 classrooms will receive the core curriculum. An additional 20 million students will be influenced by the D.A.R.E. components of kindergarten through fourth grade visitation lessons, junior and senior high curriculums, the special education curriculum, the parent program, and the D.A.R.E. + P.L.U.S. (Play and Learn Under Supervision) afterschool activity program.

D.A.R.E. is taught by law enforcement officers in nineteen countries and is being implemented in Department of Defense Dependent Schools worldwide.

From "Drug Abuse Resistance Education (D.A.R.E.)," *Bureau of Justice Assistance Fact Sheet*, #NCJ FS000039, September 1995.

Program Objectives

The primary goals of D.A.R.E. are to prevent substance abuse among schoolchildren and help them develop effective gang and violence resistance techniques. The core curriculum targets young children to prepare them to avoid substance abuse and violence as they enter adolescence. D.A.R.E. lessons focus on the following objectives for all children:

- Acquiring the knowledge and skills to recognize and resist peer pressure to experiment with tobacco, alcohol, and other drugs.
- Enhancing self-esteem.
- Learning assertiveness techniques.
- Learning about positive alternatives to substance use.
- Learning anger management and conflict resolution skills.
- Developing risk assessment and decisionmaking skills.
- Reducing violence.
- Building interpersonal and communications skills.
- Resisting gang involvement.

D.A.R.E. achieves these objectives by training carefully selected law enforcement officers to teach a structured, sequential curriculum in the schools. An important byproduct of D.A.R.E. is the impact made by these uniformed officers, who work onsite in the classroom, as positive role models for the students. In addition, in every component except the parent program, a certified teacher is required to be present at all times as an active participant in the D.A.R.E. program.

D.A.R.E. Curriculum

The D.A.R.E. curriculum is continuously enhanced and expanded to more effectively meet the needs of children. Following are the current D.A.R.E. components.

Core Curriculum. Delivered by a D.A.R.E. officer to fifth and sixth grade students, the core curriculum includes one lesson each week for seventeen consecutive weeks. A number of teaching techniques are used, including question-and-answer sessions, group discussions, role-playing, and workbook exercises.

> *"The D.A.R.E. curriculum is designed to equip . . . students with the appropriate skills to resist substance abuse, violence, and gangs."*

Kindergarten Through Fourth Grade Visitation Lessons. As time permits, officers teaching the core curriculum can visit students in each of the lower grades to introduce younger students to the D.A.R.E. concept. The fifteen- to twenty-minute lessons cover such topics as obeying laws, personal safety, and the helpful and harmful uses of medicines and drugs.

Junior High Curriculum. The D.A.R.E. junior high curriculum emphasizes information and skills that enable students to resist peer pressure and negative influences in making personal choices. The ten lessons concentrate on helping students manage their feelings of anger and aggression and on showing them how to resolve conflicts without resorting to violence or to the use of alcohol or drugs.

Senior High Curriculum. The D.A.R.E. senior high curriculum focuses on the everyday situations that high school students encounter. For the first five lessons, a D.A.R.E. officer and a high school teacher use the technique of team teaching. They emphasize information and skills that enable students to act in their own best interests when facing high-risk, low-gain choices and to handle feelings of anger properly without causing harm to themselves or others. Five followup lessons, presented by the teacher, serve to reinforce the initial lessons.

> *"An important byproduct of D.A.R.E. is the impact made by these uniformed officers . . . as positive role models for the students."*

Special Education Curriculum. The D.A.R.E. Midwestern Regional Training Center, administered by the Illinois State Police, has adapted the D.A.R.E. curriculum for special populations. D.A.R.E. officers receive specialized training that prepares them to teach the seventeen-week core curriculum in special classrooms to children with learning disabilities and behavioral disorders.

Parent Component. The D.A.R.E. parent component was developed to address the growing need for comprehensive family support and involvement in school programs. It is intended for any adult interested in ensuring health, safety, and development of life skills for children. The program provides information on communication and self-esteem building, risk factors associated with young children, basic facts on drug usage and the stages of adolescent chemical dependency, protective factors and sources of pressure, violence and conflict resolution, and agency networking in the community. The sessions offer participants the opportunity to become more involved in D.A.R.E. and give them access to community resources. The program consists of six two-hour sessions, usually held in the evening, that are conducted by a certified D.A.R.E. officer.

D.A.R.E. + P.L.U.S. Component. This component was initiated in 1993 on a pilot basis at Marina del Rio School in Los Angeles, California. It was created as an extension of the successful D.A.R.E. program and is designed to help sixth, seventh, and eighth graders stay involved in school and away from gangs, drugs, and violence. D.A.R.E. + P.L.U.S. provides students with a wide range of educational, vocational, and recreational afterschool activities in a safe and well-supervised campus setting.

Critical Program Elements

The following twelve elements are considered essential for the creation of a successful D.A.R.E. program.

Joint planning. Involvement and collaboration of law enforcement and education agencies should begin early in the planning process.

Written agreement. Law enforcement and education agencies should establish a contract that spells out mutual commitment, respective police and school roles, and partnership responsibility.

Officer selection. The officer selection process should involve screening and police–school panel interviews of officer candidates.

Officer training. Intensive seminars should be jointly conducted at accredited training centers by specially trained law enforcement and education personnel.

Curriculum. The tested and validated D.A.R.E. curriculum should be faithfully replicated.

Classroom instruction. Classroom instruction should follow the format described and should be taught by trained law enforcement officers, with assistance from certified teachers.

> *"[A July 1993 Gallup Poll Survey] showed that more than 90 percent of the graduates felt that D.A.R.E. assisted them in avoiding drugs and alcohol."*

Officer appraisal. Procedures that monitor and assess an officer's classroom performance should be established.

Informal officer-student interaction. The program should include time for the officer to interact informally with the students on the playground, in the cafeteria, and at student assemblies.

Teacher orientation. At the beginning of the school year, an orientation should be conducted in which the D.A.R.E. officer familiarizes teachers with the D.A.R.E. curriculum and explains officer and teacher roles.

Inservice training. Continued officer training should be provided to ensure effectiveness, accuracy, and currency in teaching strategies.

Parent education. Each semester, a parent education evening should be held in which the D.A.R.E. officer explains the program and gives parents the opportunity to review the curriculum. In addition, a parent component, as outlined earlier, should be developed.

Community presentations. Police, educators, and others committed to the success of the D.A.R.E. effort should meet with groups from all segments of the community to promote understanding and support. . . .

Program Assessment

D.A.R.E. is the largest and most widely implemented drug and violence prevention program in the world. It has become recognized as a key element of community-based policing efforts.

In July 1993, a Gallup Poll Survey of more than 2,000 D.A.R.E. graduates was conducted. The results showed that more than 90 percent of the graduates felt that D.A.R.E. assisted them in avoiding drugs and alcohol. The program also was credited with increasing self-esteem and ability to deal with peer pressure. Graduates reported that they had used one or two of the avoidance techniques taught to them by their D.A.R.E. officers.

More recently, in 1994, a research study sponsored by the National Institute of Justice and conducted by the Research Triangle Institute indicated that D.A.R.E. is "currently our Nation's predominant school-based prevention program, and both its prevalence and popularity continue to expand." The appeal of D.A.R.E. cuts across racial, ethnic, and socioeconomic lines, and student receptivity to D.A.R.E. was rated higher than for other prevention programs. D.A.R.E. is strongly supported by school staff, students, parents, and the community. Ratings of other substance abuse prevention programs were also high, but approval of D.A.R.E. was substantially stronger.

On the basis of continual assessments and feedback from the field, the D.A.R.E. program has been expanded to a full continuum of curricula offering training to children in kindergarten through twelfth grade, so that the lessons learned in earlier grades are reinforced as students encounter peer pressure to become involved in drugs, alcohol, and high-risk behavior. The D.A.R.E. curriculum also has been revised to be more interactive through promoting active participation by students.

Drug Abuse Resistance Education May Not Work

by Jeff Elliott

About the author: *Jeff Elliott is a freelance writer.*

The October 1994 government flyer seemed like sweet vindication to the thousands of parents, police, and teachers who supported the Drug Abuse Resistance Education Program, better known by the acronym DARE. "The D.A.R.E. Program: A Review of Prevalence, User Satisfaction, and Effectiveness," the headline on the single page boasted, describing a new study of the drug-education program. More happy news followed. "Not only is DARE widespread and popular, but demand for it is high," read the flyer. DARE's ". . . appeal cuts across racial, ethnic, and socioeconomic lines [with] considerable support for expansion of the program."

Success and Criticism for DARE

Sweet vindication indeed. Since its inception in 1983, the DARE curriculum had rapidly spread from the Los Angeles area to schools across the country. In fact, more than half of all schools in the United States currently use the program; almost 20 million schoolkids a year are visited at least once by a DARE instructor. Despite such success, however, critics had been increasingly vocal in recent years, attacking the program as a costly and ineffective way of teaching kids about the perils of drug abuse. They claimed that DARE was just another untested pedagogical gimmick that served no purpose other than soaking up private donations and local, state, and federal tax dollars.

The newly released study, then, would simultaneously silence naysayers while boosting DARE's shot at more public funds and deeper penetration into schools. This is no penny-ante business, either: DARE, which was specifically held up as exemplary in two sections of the 1994 crime bill, is competing with other drug-ed programs for a chunk of the more than $500 million the feds put aside for such instruction. And running DARE takes a lot of money. A DARE spokesperson claims the program costs somewhat less than $200 million annually, but other credible estimates range as high as $700 million, once all costs are considered.

The claims in the government flyer were accurate—to a point. The three-year study, commissioned by the National Institute of Justice (NIJ), the research office for the U.S. Department of Justice, did include those observations. Researchers found that DARE raises children's self-esteem, polishes their social skills, and improves their attitudes toward police.

But unfortunately for DARE boosters, the study also proved something else: DARE doesn't have a measurable effect on drug abuse. While the flyer devoted ample space to puffery, it dismissed the critical heart of the study in just two terse sentences. And it did not mention that NIJ had refused to publish the study, despite positive peer review.

A Faulty Research Study?

Charges and countercharges flew throughout the early weeks of October. NIJ was trying to put a positive spin on bad news and suppressing the study, claimed DARE critics. Not so, NIJ Director Jeremy Travis replied in one letter to the editor: Questions about "the scientific validity" of the study were raised by NIJ reviewers, and the work did not meet their "high standards of methodological rigor."

Travis's letter was a stinging rebuke to the prestigious Research Triangle Institute (RTI), which has authored hundreds of government studies without complaint. Under pressure to withdraw the study or rewrite the conclusions, the scientists stood by their work. "We agreed to disagree," says principal author Susan Ennett.

Accusations of faulty research trouble Ennett and her co-authors, who point out that ongoing government reviews examined their work in progress. "We worked with NIJ throughout, sending drafts and getting back comments," says Ennett. "[The review] didn't just happen at the end." Ennett says there were four outside reviews over the lifetime of the three-year project, as well as in-house reviews by NIJ itself.

> *"DARE doesn't have a measurable effect on drug abuse."*

Another curious aspect of the government reaction is that the RTI study contained no original research. Only previously published studies were examined, and all had reached the same dismal conclusions about DARE. Says Ennett, "The results of all the studies used in the meta-analysis were consistent; it's not like the conclusions of these different studies were all over the place. We did not find any support for [a statistically significant] impact on drug use, and they show DARE has no effect at all on marijuana use." Another author of the study is more blunt: "The kids learn to have respect for police: fine and dandy. But if it's sold for the prevention of drug use, it's not working."

But even if NIJ had signed off on the study, the government had another excuse ready: A new, improved DARE was introduced in the autumn of 1994. And, as the flyer noted, "The effects of the new curriculum on learning and behavior may in turn call for a new evaluation." In the eyes of the Justice Department, in other words, all the research that proves DARE ineffective is now invalid.

This position infuriates many researchers, who view it as a disingenuous attempt to deflect criticism. Claiming that a revised program is entirely new is a well-known academic shell game. "There's not a new curriculum—there's a slightly changed curriculum," argues Richard Clayton, director of the Center of Prevention Research at the University of Kentucky. Clayton, who is now concluding a five-year evaluation of DARE in Kentucky, says his findings also match the conclusions in the RTI study.

"I'm really not surprised NIJ refused to publish it," says Clayton, "but I'm disappointed. DARE has a leadership role to play because it's in half the schools. An organization that receives that much public funding has an obligation to be honest with the public.". . .

In the DARE Classroom

DARE Officer Terry Campbell is on stage. It is the first time he has visited this fourth-grade class, but most of the children already know him well. As the full-time DARE instructor for Petaluma, California, he has been in the classrooms since 1988. One of the program's recent graduates was Polly Klaas, whose abduction and murder [in October 1993] brought sad fame to this small town, forty-five minutes north of San Francisco.

After he introduces himself, the twenty-minute lesson begins. Campbell asks if anyone knows what DARE means and a girl is quick to respond, "Drug Abuse Resistance Education."

> *"The kids learn to have respect for police: fine and dandy. But if it's sold for the prevention of drug use, it's not working."*

"What's a drug?" Campbell asks. The kids have ready answers, a mix of formal names and common slang. Cocaine. Alcohol. Tobacco. Coke. Pot.

"I know a different kind of drug," a boy adds. "It's a medicine."

Campbell asks, "What is it?"

"Penicillin." The officer asks if his parents ever gave him Children's Tylenol for a headache. Yes, they have.

"Did you take it in the right way?"

"Yes."

"Today, maybe you have a bad headache. Should you take 10 Tylenol?"

"No," the children chorus.

"That's right. That's called drug abuse. That's all a drug is—something that can help you or hurt you, depending on how you take it."

The children listen attentively. Campbell is more than a police officer; he is also a natural teacher, demonstrating a genius that outreaches mere talent. In front of a class, he is transformed, riffing off the kids' questions and comments like Robin Williams, connecting with every child in the room. Hands down, he is one of the best teachers imaginable. DARE and the city of Petaluma are fortunate.

In all classes, time is set aside for questions. Before school, Campbell accurately predicted the first question: "Have you ever shot anybody?" Simi-

> *"Kids don't relate to national or state data. . . . It's what their friends are doing that counts."*

lar career-day questions follow as the intrigued fourth graders quiz their visiting policeman. His profession is close to their minds; like all DARE officers, Campbell wears his uniform—but sans handgun, walkie-talkie, and other tools of his trade.

The Core Curriculum

These brief kindergarten through fifth-grade classroom visits, Campbell later explains, lay the groundwork for the DARE core curriculum, taught in the sixth grade. Campbell gives safety advice, reminds them to call 911 "if they need to," and prepares them for their DARE sessions. Not insignificantly, he also becomes a familiar and trusted figure. "One of the most beneficial things of the program is that kids get to see police officers like human beings," he says, corroborating a finding of the NIJ-sponsored study.

Next in his schedule is a sixth-grade DARE lesson, where Campbell teaches the fourth of the seventeen lessons in the DARE curriculum. It opens with one of the most controversial elements of the program: the DARE Box. On a window shelf rests the decorated shoebox, where anonymous notes can be passed to Campbell.

Campbell reads the first question: "Someone in my family is doing drugs and I'm worried that if I say anything it will make it worse." Heads spin. Who is it?

"Don't look around," Campbell says quickly. "It isn't important to know who wrote it."

A girl raises her hand. "Maybe that kid wants to talk to you about it."

"I'm more than willing to do that," he smiles warmly. "You all know me." He asks them the consequences of using an illegal drug.

"You could get in trouble," one child says. Another adds, "You could die."

Says Campbell, "It's probably OK to get them into trouble, if that's going to happen."

A boy asks, "What if it's one of your parents?"

"You should talk to a teacher or a counselor, or another adult you trust." As Campbell begins the lesson proper, he slips the note into his pocket.

Of the twenty-seven children in this class, only the boy who apparently asked the question does not immediately open his workbook. Instead, he toys with the paper nameplate sitting on his desk. On the side of the wide triangle facing him are printed the eight ways to say no as taught by DARE. On the opposite side—the side facing Campbell—is the child's name.

What happened to the note? "I threw it away," Campbell says later. "But I didn't put it in the wastebasket in the classroom because one of the kids could find out who wrote it." Campbell was occupied with preparing for the lesson and didn't notice the nervous boy. Still, he says he wouldn't have acted on it if he had. "First, we don't know if they were illegal drugs—it could be alcohol or tobacco. Secondly, I may have a feeling that a child is having problems, but I can't make that assumption. Maybe he was fidgeting because he needed to go to the bathroom."

Several times in the last six years, Campbell has found signed notes in the DARE Box. "If a child wrote that he was being abused or in danger, of course I would follow up on it." Recently, he received a note indicating child abuse. "I got the child appropriate help," says Campbell.

The 14 Percent Solution

"How many of you think people will actually force you to use drugs?" Campbell asks, bringing Maggie, one of the girls in the class, to the front of the room. (The names of the children have been changed.) "It's possible that somebody's gonna hold a gun to your head and say, take these drugs. More common is the form that Maggie and I have been best friends since kindergarten and I say, 'Hey, Maggie, I got some marijuana here and I think it's really great'. . ."

"NO!" the child interrupts loudly, with a self-conscious giggle.

". . . Would you like to try it?"

"NO!"

"Come on, we won't be best friends if you don't."

"NO!"

It is the introduction to a lesson on peer pressure and leads into a discussion of how friends can subtly coax agreement. Campbell reads from the DARE workbook: "How many seventh-grade students out of 100 have been drunk from any alcoholic beverage?" The children, organized into groups of five and six, are to come up with a collective answer.

> *"It's important for kids to know that drug abuse is the exception rather than the norm."*

More than a little confusion spreads through the classroom about the assignment. The workbook explains this is the result of a "recent national survey," but many don't understand what that means. Does it include New York? one child asks. San Jose? A couple of minutes pass as the children struggle to understand what they are asked to do.

As the groups debate, Campbell wanders through the room, eavesdropping. Just as he approaches, one of the groups settles on 17.5 percent. A girl writes the number in her workbook as Campbell peers over her shoulder. She looks to him for approval but he says nothing, and his face remains blank. As he moves to the next group, she turns to classmates: "Let's go a little bit higher; he didn't seem to like that."

The five groups come to five different solutions, ranging between 42 percent and 70 percent. Campbell smiles; the exercise has worked. The correct answer, he reveals, is 14 percent. He points to the group that first had a 17.5 percent answer. He overheard one boy vote for 15 percent but relent against the collective will of the group. "This demonstrates how peer pressure

> *"By 1991, there were more than a dozen studies that claimed DARE didn't work at all."*

works," Campbell says. "We allowed our peers to talk us into it. Is everybody out there doing drugs?"

The class chimes no, in unison.

"Just because somebody does it doesn't mean everybody does. Did I surprise you that the figure was so low?" Campbell asks.

"No," the class responds again, but weaker.

Faulty Lesson Designs

Unfortunately, the 14 percent statistic used in the lesson is incorrect. And it's not even from a recent nationwide survey—the number comes from research done between 1989 and 1990 in California alone. The survey is done every two years for the state attorney general, and the most recent figure for seventh graders who have ever been intoxicated is 23 percent.

Even though DARE's statistic is wrong it is still lower than any of the estimates by the children. The objective of the lesson is valid; childhood perceptions of normal behavior can be badly skewed.

More troublesome is the lesson design. Only a wrong answer is "right"; the lesson fails if the class picks accurate numbers. When one group chose 17.5 percent, Campbell—probably unconsciously—led them to raise their guesstimate by implying disapproval. Such subtle problems with design can give even brilliant teachers like Campbell fits.

Shown a transcript of this session, researchers not associated with DARE agree that the point of the lesson was valuable but dismiss the DARE exercise as useless. "Kid's don't relate to national or state data," says Joel Moskowitz, who has authored evaluations of several drug education programs. "It's what their friends are doing that counts."

Moskowitz and others were also critical of the role-playing between Campbell and Maggie. "It should have been between two adolescents," Moskowitz says. "She just parroted the lines the police officer expected. It's not going to be so easy to say no to a friend if it's going to make them your enemy."

As the primary author of the DARE curriculum, Dr. Ruth Rich responds to their criticism. "The problem with this lesson is that the kids don't understand the math," she says. Not so, at least in Petaluma. The children in this class actually skidded to a halt over the concept of a nationwide survey. The same confusion was repeated in another sixth-grade class, later in the day. If the point of the lesson is to teach kids that not everyone does drugs and "that concept is not being taught, we need to work on it," Rich concedes.

What about the complaint that a peer should have played the role of the friend offering Maggie drugs? Says Rich, "We have the officers role-play with the youngsters. We try to get the situation as real as possible, but we would never have a child offering a joint—it reinforces the negative."

The problems with this lesson demonstrate something else as well: Designing an effective anti-drug program ain't easy.

When Maggie role-plays saying no to Officer Campbell, she reinforces her skills at turning down drugs from a uniformed policeman. Not a likely real-life scenario. But if Maggie rejects a reefer from classmate Tommy, Maggie has a more realistic experience—and Tommy gets some practice in pushing drugs.

Similarly, it's important for kids to know that drug abuse is the exception rather than the norm. Is there a better solution than the troublesome "national survey" question? . . .

The Emperor's Clothing

DARE keeps children away from drugs. That *raison d'être* sold thousands of communities on the program and keeps DARE in the schools, even if budget cuts must be made somewhere else. But by 1991, there were more than a dozen studies that claimed DARE didn't work at all. Not that it was useless: It had positive effects on children's knowledge about drugs, helped develop their social skills, and improved their attitude about police. But all these studies said the same thing about drug use—if DARE had any effect at all, it was short lived.

Except for one study: a 1986 evaluation by William DeJong, used by NIJ to start the DARE bandwagon rolling. When DeJong's research appeared in the *Journal of Drug Education*, his colleagues called the design of his study "seriously flawed." Among their complaints was that the children were given no test before starting the DARE program, which made it impossible to evaluate any claims of improvement. Critics also noted that the study revealed positive effects only with boys; there was a significant negative impact on the DARE girls—the boomerang effect.

In 1991, NIJ decided to settle the question of DARE's worth by hiring analysts at Research Triangle Institute (RTI) to do a comprehensive evaluation. To DARE, it seemed like vindication and due respect was finally at hand. "The review of the DARE evaluation literature will give us ammunition to respond to critics who charge that DARE has not proved its effectiveness," read a DARE letter sent to state coordinators.

RTI researchers, of course, found no new ammunition for DARE in the studies. Yes, the program improved the relationship between schoolchildren and the police, and taught the kids many useful things. But as far as stopping them from using drugs . . . sorry.

Parents Should Not Rely on Drug Testing of Teenagers

by Mark Frankel

About the author: *Mark Frankel is a writer for* Newsweek International *in New York City.*

With no sign that drug use is waning, a Massachusetts company is promising to provide a quick fix for those who think rigorous monitoring is an answer. The Psychemedics Corporation of Cambridge has begun selling anxious parents a no-muss, no-fuss way to test their kids for drug use without ever leaving their home.

Playing on Parents' Fear

Introduced in July 1995, the firm's PDT-90 Personal Drug Testing Service was unveiled with a fear-mongering newspaper ad headlined "An Open Letter to the Parents of America," which deftly played upon parental dread ("Even if you do everything right, your child might still try drugs. A third of eighth graders in the U.S. has used drugs. One-half of twelfth graders has," it read in part.) Parents were invited to call Psychemedics's toll-free number to order one of the $75 test packets. For their cash, they received a company-supplied envelope, along with instructions on how to clip and deposit a small lock of their child's hair inside it, to be mailed for analysis at Psychemedics's lab in Culver City, California. The company has patented a technique that it claims can detect evidence of drug use by analyzing no more than four or five dozen strands of hair. Within a few weeks' time, Psychemedics promises to provide a confidential report on its test results.

Fear sells. Psychemedics executives refuse to say how many PDT-90 packets they have peddled so far, but company president Raymond Kubacki says the initial response has been "overwhelming" for a product still in the early stages of test-marketing. He is particularly upbeat about the reaction generated by direct-mail ads that were sent to 13,000 high school drug counselors.

From Mark Frankel, "Mom and Pop Test for Drugs," *Nation*, January 29, 1996. Reprinted with permission from the *Nation* magazine; © The Nation Company, L.P.

Pushing aside the obvious civil liberties concerns for a moment, there's another reason parents should hesitate before grabbing the nearest shears and asking their kids to please step into the bathroom. "Hair testing is not always correct, nor a perfect measure," says Dr. Edward Cone, chief of chemistry and drug metabolism at the Addiction Research Center in Baltimore, Maryland, part of the National Institutes of Health (NIH). "There are a lot of problems that have not been fully explored or explained." The Food and Drug Administration (FDA) has pointedly refused to approve the test method, having described it as "an unproven procedure unsupported by the scientific literature or well-controlled studies and clinical trials." The Society of Forensic Toxicologists has also refused to endorse it as a stand-alone test for drugs. And a Nevada judge ruled in 1990 that hair analysis alone "has not . . . developed sufficiently to form a basis for termination of current employees" for drug use. Urinalysis remains the legal and scientific standard for drug testing.

Widespread Use of the Test

That has not stopped Psychemedics's powerful backers and their political allies from lobbying assiduously for government approval. Nor has it prevented about 500 companies, including such household names as Blockbuster Entertainment, from relying upon Psychemedics's dubious hair testing to screen job applicants. "These guys don't know much about science, but they have done an incredible marketing job," says J. Michael Walsh, the former director of applied research at the National Institute for Drug Abuse (NIDA). At stake is a $750 million market, which is now dominated by urinalysis labs.

Indeed, word of PDT-90's rollout ignited a small stampede on Wall Street: Psychemedics's share price tripled to more than $10 a share in only a few days. And in early November 1995, Psychemedics teamed up with swaggering New Orleans District Attorney Harry Connick, who proposed employing Psychemedics to test the city's public high school students for drugs. Citing a June 1995 U.S. Supreme Court ruling that permits drug testing of public school athletes, Connick proposed launching a one-year pilot program at two city high schools; if successful, hair testing would then be expanded to all 21,000 secondary students in the system. Appearing at a news conference with Connick, Kubacki said his company would underwrite the cost of the pilot program. If a citywide program is implemented however, parents could expect to pick up the $50-per-pupil tab themselves. . . .

> *"Parents should hesitate before grabbing the nearest shears and asking their kids to please step into the bathroom."*

The new drug test has roots in old science. It's long been common knowledge among pathologists (as well as readers of mystery novels) that minute traces of heavy metals like arsenic wind up in hair after ingestion. Working in Los Angeles in the late seventies, Dr. Werner Baumgartner, an Austrian-born chemist, reasoned that hair could also be utilized to screen for drugs. By breaking down hair proteins and using radioimmunoassay, Baumgartner claimed he could detect marijuana, cocaine, opiates, amphetamine or PCP in amounts as small as one-billionth of a gram.

Proponents of hair testing claim the technique has two great advantages over conventional urinalysis. First, it eliminates the dripping specimen cups and embarrassment that go

> *"New Orleans District Attorney Harry Connick . . . proposed employing Psychemedics to test the city's public high school students for drugs."*

along with "Fill this cup and leave it on the back of the toilet." Second, traces of most street drugs are purged from the body after only two or three days. Psychemedics, on the other hand, claims its hair-test methods provide a "window of detection" that will spot any drug use ninety days prior to testing. That sales line has proved irresistible to the more than 500 companies that have employed Psychemedics to screen their workers for drug use. Clients include the MGM Grand Hotel in Las Vegas, Steelcase Corporation and Harrah's casinos, though by far the largest single customer has been Blockbuster, the entertainment conglomerate Huizenga sold to Viacom in 1994.

While the Psychemedics executives insist that its tests are "100 percent accurate," that depends on whose research you read. Plenty of studies do not support such brimming confidence. The biggest question mark is the precise mechanism by which cocaine is absorbed into the hair. While some traces are absorbed from the bloodstream, there's also evidence that cocaine might be absorbed by hair from sweat and sebum, the greasy coating produced by the scalp. In one study at the University of California, Davis, Medical School, the husband-and-wife team of Gary Henderson and Martha Harkey found significant levels of cocaine showing up in clean hair samples that had merely been handled by test subjects who had received measured doses of cocaine intravenously or intranasally. Thus it is difficult to determine whether hair has been externally contaminated or tainted by ingestion.

The Trouble with Hair Testing

Anyone who has whiffed tobacco smoke in their hair hours after leaving a smoky cocktail party knows how readily hair traps airborne particles. Two-thirds of the thirty-five children (many of them age eight or younger) living in homes in which crack was smoked routinely were found to have cocaine in their hair, according to a study conducted at the University of Alabama, Birmingham. Some of the kids had higher levels of drug residue in their hair than adults living under the same roof. "If one assumes that young children are not intentional cocaine users, these results show that their hair can become cocaine positive through passive exposure," concluded the study abstract. Fred Smith, a co-author of the study, says, "I was a proponent of hair testing until I started looking at reports." There's also some evidence that test results are skewed by the subject's race or gender. Animal research done at the Center for Human Toxicology at the University of Utah indicates that darkly pigmented hair containing high levels of melanin accumulates more cocaine residue than lighter colored hair. Lastly, another study by the center raises the possibility that women's hair might hold more drug residue than men's.

Twelve-Step Programs Can Help Teenagers Overcome Addiction

by Tammy Bell

About the author: *Tammy Bell is the director of the Relapse Prevention Center in Charlotte, North Carolina.*

Poor recovery rates for chemically dependent adolescents have continuously plagued the field of addictions treatment. Once we finally get adolescents to understand that they are chemically dependent and need to get sober, the real work begins.

Why, after receiving the same type of treatment as adults, do the adolescents fail to stay sober? This question requires a multi-faceted response. Everything from lack of community resources to environment, parental absence, limited and overmanaged treatment dollars, and the immaturity of the population itself contribute to poor adolescent recovery rates.

Alone in Sobriety

One major factor contributing to adolescent relapse has been the adolescent's inability to develop a sobriety-centered social life and/or lifestyle. My experience with recovering adolescents is that leaving the "old life" of parties, paraphernalia, war stories, excitement, and companionship is quite difficult.

However, giving up a social life completely just doesn't seem to work for adolescents. Recovering adolescents often feel alienated, alone, and uncomfortable in sobriety. Often, some of this discomfort is caused by simply being away from things that are familiar. Most of it, however, is derived from the adolescents' strong internal drive to connect to a peer group for support as they become independent and separate from their parents or caregivers. This overwhelming need for a peer group is part of the natural developmental process during the adolescent years and it does not go away during recovery.

Tammy Bell, "Staying Sober: Focus on Sobriety Is Essential," *Professional Counselor*, June 1996. Copyright © 1996, Health Communications Inc. Reprinted by permission of Health Communications Inc.

I have seen little evidence that most treatment programs recognize this important need in the adolescent world. First and foremost, they are adolescents. If recovery is to have a chance to work in their lives, we must find a way for chemically dependent adolescents to enter a new peer culture as smoothly as possible. Failure to do this will result in a natural tendency to return to what's familiar (old friends).

> *"Leaving the 'old life' of parties, paraphernalia, war stories, excitement, and companionship is quite difficult [for adolescents]."*

Although chemically dependent adolescents need 12-step programs such as Alcoholics Anonymous and Narcotics Anonymous, they often do not like attending AA/NA meetings. Many of the adults in these programs do not like adolescents either.

Effective Methods

Twelve-step programs are abstract and adolescents would rather deal with concrete, easy-to-understand concepts. They can become confused and overwhelmed by 12-step principles. When adolescents become overwhelmed, boredom results. For those of you who know anything about children, boredom is outranked only by pain in the top-10 list of things to be avoided.

In spite of the obvious obstacles to uniting AA and adolescents, here are some effective methods. At the beginning:

1. Don't send kids to AA/NA meetings, escort them.
2. Know which meetings will welcome and respect adolescents and avoid the ones that don't.
3. Prepare adolescents for the meetings, educationally and emotionally, before they attend one.
4. Go to the extra trouble of introducing them to younger recovering people (at least under thirty-five years old).
5. Select their first temporary sponsor from a list of AA/NA volunteers.
6. Have them quickly select and make a commitment to a home group.
7. Don't send adolescents to AA/NA until they want to go. Otherwise, it could be viewed as punishment.
8. Don't expect the adolescent's recovery to be as mature or insightful as an adult's.

Twelve-Step Meetings Can Help Adolescents

These meetings should be presented as positive and interesting experiences, not as a way to have fun. You'll just seem old and out of it if you try to convince adolescents that meetings are fun. Twelve-step meetings are a good place for recovering adolescents to spend time, feel supported, and grapple with this abstract concept of recovery. They are not a replacement for an age-appropriate peer group, which is critical to recovery for the adolescent.

The adolescent's counselor, parents, and AA/NA associates should spend a good deal of time helping the adolescent meet and interact with other teenagers.

It is important to help recovering adolescents, whose addiction temporarily has disrupted their normal lives, to rejoin their regularly scheduled life, which is already in progress.

Chapter 4

Can Regulation of Tobacco Marketing Prevent Teenage Addiction to Cigarettes?

CURRENT CONTROVERSIES

Chapter Preface

Since 1993, the U.S. Food and Drug Administration (FDA) has been studying the possibility of regulating nicotine in tobacco as an addictive drug. The agency has been particularly concerned with combating nicotine addiction among juveniles. To prevent minors from obtaining cigarettes, in August 1996 the FDA instituted new rules concerning tobacco sales and advertising. Included in the new measures is a controversial ban on promotional items such as t-shirts and caps sporting cigarette brand logos, which are usually given away in exchange for proofs of purchase from cigarette packages.

Anti-tobacco activists applaud the FDA rules, arguing that they are necessary to reverse the increase in teenage smoking that has occurred in the 1990s. John F. Banzhaf III, executive director of Action on Smoking and Health (ASH), attributes the increase in teenage smoking to the marketing and promotional giveaways used by cigarette makers to lure young adults. "Kids get a desire to own one of these products," Banzhaf says. In order to send away for the caps and t-shirts, he points out, they have to get the proofs of purchases from cigarette packages. "That tends to break down the aversion [to smoking]," he argues. Banzhaf and other critics maintain that because tobacco industry promotions are intentionally designed to entice teenagers to become smokers, the FDA regulations are necessary to prevent teens from obtaining cigarettes and becoming addicted.

Tobacco supporters both inside and outside the industry criticize the FDA rules as heavy-handed. Thomas Lauria, spokesman for the Tobacco Institute, the national lobby of the tobacco industry, characterizes the regulations as the first step in a campaign by the FDA to impose the prohibition of tobacco. Daniel L. Jaffe, executive vice president of the Association of National Advertisers, also believes that the FDA rules are too restrictive. "While we agree the government should have authority to protect children," Jaffe states, "we feel it has gone way beyond that legitimate goal by trying to impose restrictions that would make it virtually impossible to advertise [cigarettes] to anybody." Jaffe and Lauria maintain that cigarette promotions are aimed at adult smokers, not at teenagers. They argue that the FDA measures unnecessarily restrict tobacco advertising and will not affect teen smoking rates at all.

While anti-tobacco activists hope that the FDA regulations on tobacco promotions will reduce tobacco use among teenagers, critics contend that the rules are too heavy-handed and will ultimately be ineffectual. The viewpoints in the following chapter represent opinions on both sides of the debate.

FDA Regulation of Tobacco May Be Necessary to Prevent Teenage Addiction

by David A. Kessler

About the author: *David A. Kessler is commissioner of the Food and Drug Administration.*

The tobacco industry has argued that the decision to smoke and continue to smoke is a free choice made by an adult. But ask a smoker when he or she began to smoke. Chances are you will hear the tale of a child.

Cigarette Addiction Begins in Childhood

It's the age-old story, kids sneaking away to experiment with tobacco, trying to smoke without coughing, without getting dizzy, and staring at themselves in a mirror just to see how smooth and sophisticated they can look.

The child learns the ritual. It is a ritual born partly out of a childish curiosity, partly out of a youthful need to rebel, partly out of a need to feel accepted, and wholly without regard for danger. It is a ritual that often, tragically, lasts a lifetime. And it is a ritual that can cut short that lifetime.

Many of us picture youngsters simply experimenting with cigarettes. They try smoking like they try out the latest fad—and often drop it just as quickly. But when you recognize that many young people progress steadily from experimentation to regular use, with addiction taking hold within a few years, the image is far different, far more disconcerting. Between one-third and one-half of adolescents who try smoking even a few cigarettes soon become regular smokers.

What is perhaps most striking is that young people who start smoking soon regret it. Seven out of ten who smoke report that they regret ever having started. But like adults, they have enormous difficulty quitting. Certainly some succeed, but three out of four young smokers have tried to quit at least once and failed.

Consider the experience of one sixteen-year-old girl, quoted in *Parade* maga-

From David A. Kessler, remarks given at the Samuel Rubin Program, the Columbia University School of Law, New York, N.Y., March 8, 1995.

zine in December 1994. She started to smoke when she was eight because her older brother smoked. Today, she says: "Now, I'm stuck. I can't quit. . . . It's so incredibly bad to nic-fit, it's not even funny. When your body craves the nicotine, it's just: 'I need a cigarette.'"

In her own terms she has summarized the scientific findings of the 1988 Surgeon General's report, *The Health Consequences of Smoking, Nicotine Addiction*. That report concluded: "Cigarettes and other forms of tobacco are addicting" and "Nicotine is the drug in tobacco that causes addiction."

Let there be no doubt that nicotine is an addictive substance. Many studies have documented the presence of the key addiction criteria relied on by major medical organizations. These criteria include: highly controlled or compulsive use, even despite a desire or repeated attempts to quit; psychoactive effects on the brain; and drug-motivated behavior caused by the "reinforcing" effects of the psychoactive substance. Quitting episodes followed by relapse and withdrawal symptoms that can motivate further use are some additional criteria of an addictive substance.

Teens Underestimate the Risk of Addiction

Are young people simply unaware of the dangers associated with smoking and nicotine addiction? No, not really. They just do not believe that these dangers apply to them.

For healthy young people, death and illness are just distant rumors. And until they experience the grip of nicotine addiction for themselves, they vastly underestimate its power over them. They are young, they are fearless, and they are confident that they will be able to quit smoking when they want to, and certainly well before any adverse health consequences occur.

"Between one-third and one-half of adolescents who try smoking even a few cigarettes soon become regular smokers."

They are also wrong. We see that documented in papers acquired from one tobacco company in a Canadian court case. A study prepared for the company called "Project 16" describes how the typical youthful experimenter becomes an addicted smoker within a few years.

> However intriguing smoking was at 11, 12, or 13, by the age of 16 or 17 many regretted their use of cigarettes for health reasons and because they feel unable to stop smoking when they want to. . . . Over half claim they want to quit. However, they cannot quit any easier than adults can.

This sense of helplessness and regret was further tracked in a subsequent study for the company called "Project Plus/Minus." It was completed in 1982:

> [T]he desire to quit seems to come earlier now than ever before, even prior to the end of high school. In fact, it often seems to take hold as soon as the recent starter admits to himself that he is hooked on smoking. However, the desire to quit and actually carrying it out, are two quite different things, as the would-be quitter soon learns.

Teen Smoking Is Increasing

Unfortunately, youth smoking gives no sign of abating. While the prevalence of smoking among adults has steadily declined since 1964, the prevalence of smoking by young people stalled for more than a decade and recently has begun to rise. Between 1992 and 1993 the prevalence of smoking by high school seniors increased from 17.2 percent to 19 percent. Smoking among college freshmen rose from 9 percent in 1985 to 12.5 percent in 1994.

And young people's addiction to nicotine is not limited to smoking. Children's use of smokeless tobacco, such as snuff and chewing tobacco, is also extensive. Today, of the seven million people in this country who use smokeless tobacco, as many as one in four is under the age of nineteen.

This epidemic of youth addiction to nicotine has enormous public health consequences. A casual decision at a young age to use tobacco products can lead to addiction, serious disease, and premature death as an adult.

> *"Until [young people] experience the grip of nicotine addiction for themselves, they vastly underestimate its power over them."*

More than 400,000 smokers die each year from smoking-related illnesses.

Smoking kills more people each year in the United States than AIDS, car accidents, alcohol, homicides, illegal drugs, suicides and fires combined. And the real tragedy is that these deaths from smoking are preventable.

In 1994 the Food and Drug Administration (FDA) raised the question of whether the Agency has a role in preventing this problem. FDA has responsibility for the drugs, devices, biologics and food used in this country. Since 1994 we have been looking at whether nicotine-containing tobacco products are drugs subject to the requirements of the Federal Food, Drug, and Cosmetic Act. Our study continues. But we already know this: Nicotine is an addictive substance and the marketplace for tobacco products is sustained by this addiction. And what is striking is that it is young people who are becoming addicted.

Tobacco Companies Know Nicotine Is Addictive

Statements from internal documents by industry researchers and executives show that they understood that nicotine is addictive and how important it is to their product. Listen to these statements made decades ago:

> We are, then, in the business of selling nicotine, an addictive drug.

—Addison Yeaman, general counsel, Brown & Williamson Tobacco Co. (1963)

> Think of the cigarette pack as a storage container for a day's supply of nicotine. Think of the cigarette as a dispenser for a dose unit of nicotine. Think of a puff of smoke as the vehicle for nicotine.

—William L. Dunn Jr., senior official, Philip Morris (1972)

And consider what a research group reported to one tobacco company about starter smokers who assume they will not become addicted:

But addicted they do indeed become.

—"Project Plus/Minus" (1982)

More recently, in November 1994, a former chief executive officer of a major American tobacco company told the *Wall Street Journal*: "Of course it's addictive. That's why you smoke. . . ." And a former smokeless tobacco industry chemist was quoted as saying: "There used to be a saying at [the company] that 'There's a hook in every can' . . . [a]nd that hook is nicotine."

Nevertheless, the industry publicly insists that smoking is a choice freely made by adults. An advertisement by one of the major tobacco companies that appeared in newspapers across the country in November 1994 bore a

> *"A casual decision at a young age to use tobacco products can lead to addiction, serious disease, and premature death as an adult."*

headline that read, "Where Exactly Is the Land of the Free?" It suggests that the government is interested in banning cigarettes—although no one in government has advocated such a position. With some 40 million smokers addicted to nicotine, a ban would not be feasible.

The ad never addresses youth smoking. And it says, "The time has come to allow adults in this country to make their own decisions of their own free will, without Government control and excessive intervention.". . .

Spending on Cigarette Advertising

We cannot adequately address this pediatric disease our country faces without recognizing the important influences on a young person's decision to smoke. One such influence is industry advertising and promotion. It is important to understand the effects of these practices on young people.

In the last two decades, the amount of money the cigarette industry has spent to advertise and promote its products has dramatically risen. Despite a long-standing ban on broadcast advertising, in 1992 alone the industry spent more than $5.2 billion. This makes it the second most heavily advertised commodity in the United States, second only to automobiles.

Tobacco advertising appears in print media, on billboards, at point of sale, by direct mail, on an array of consumer items such as hats, t-shirts, jackets, and lighters, and at concerts and sporting events. The sheer magnitude of advertising creates the impression among young people that smoking is much more ubiquitous and socially acceptable than it is. In studies, young smokers consistently overestimate the percentage of people who smoke.

In addition, tobacco industry advertising themes and images resonate with young people. Advertising experts describe the cigarette package as a "badge" product that adolescents show to create a desired self-image and to communicate that image to others. As a retired leading advertising executive has stated: "When the teenagers lose the visual link between the advertising and the point of sale . . . they will lose much of the incentive to rebel against authority and try smoking."

Since the early 1990s, the tobacco industry has been spending more money on marketing and promotion and less on traditional advertising. For example, it distributes catalogues of items that can be obtained with proof of purchase coupons attached to cigarette packs—such as Camel Cash and Marlboro Miles. These coupons are exchanged for non-tobacco consumer items imprinted with product logos.

These items have proven to be a big hit with children and adolescents. Half of all adolescent smokers and one quarter of adolescent non-smokers own at least one promotional item from a tobacco company, according to a 1992 Gallup survey.

Sponsorship of athletic, musical, sporting and other events is another important way that the industry promotes its product. This links tobacco products with the glamorous and appealing worlds of sports and entertainment. And the logos of their brands are viewed during televised events, despite the federally mandated broadcast advertising ban.

Make no mistake: All of this advertising and promotion is chillingly effective. The three most heavily advertised brands of cigarettes are Marlboro, Camel and Newport. A 1994 study by the Centers for Disease Control and Prevention found that 86 percent of underage smokers who purchase their own cigarettes purchased one of those three heavily advertised brands.

The advertisements apparently have far less impact on adults. By far, the most popular brand choices for adults are the private label, price value, and plain package brands, which rely on little or no imagery on their packaging or advertising.

The Joe Camel Campaign

Let me describe a campaign to illustrate the effects that advertising and marketing practices can have on young people. This campaign gave new life to a cigarette brand with an aging customer base. . . .

In the early 1980s, Camel cigarettes were smoked primarily by men over fifty, and commanded about 3 to 4 percent of the overall market. So the company began to make plans to reposition Camel.

> *"Statements . . . by [tobacco] industry researchers and executives show that they understood that nicotine is addictive."*

The new advertising for Camel was designed to take advantage of Camel's 75th birthday. The campaign featured the cartoon character "Joe Camel" as its anthropomorphic spokescamel who gave dating advice called "smooth moves" and who eventually was joined by a whole gang of hip camels at the watering hole.

The campaign was variously described as irreverent, humorous and sophomoric. But Joe Camel gave the company what it wanted: a new vehicle to reposition the Camel brand with more youth appeal.

During the same time period, the company devised what it called a Young Adult Smokers program—which went by the acronym YAS. The program was designed to appeal to the eighteen to twenty-four age group, and more narrowly to the eighteen- to twenty-year-old audience. The program also had a tracking system to monitor sales in these groups.

> *"Tobacco industry advertising themes and images resonate with young people."*

Let me give you several facts about that program.

First, on January 10, 1990, a division manager in Sarasota, Florida, issued a memorandum describing a method to increase the exposure and access to the Young Adult Market for the Joe Camel campaign. The memorandum asked sales representatives to identify stores within their areas that "are heavily frequented by young adult shoppers. These stores can be in close proximity to colleges [and] high schools. . . ." The purpose of the memorandum was to make sure that those stores were always stocked with items that appeal to younger people—such as hats and t-shirts—carrying the Camel name and imagery.

A May 1990 *Wall Street Journal* article revealed the contents of this letter and it also contained the company's response that the memo was a mistake. The company said the mistake had been corrected and explained that the manager had violated company policy by targeting high school students. However, on April 5, 1990, another division manager, this time in Oklahoma, sent a memo to all area sales representatives and chain service representatives in parts of Oklahoma. The memo refers to what it calls "Retail Young Adult Smoker Retailer Account[s]" and goes on to say:

> The criteria for you to utilize in identifying these accounts are as follows:
> (1) . . . calls located across from, adjacent to [or] in the general vicinity of the High Schools. . . .

Smokers and Brand Loyalty

Second, an additional element of its Camel campaign was known as FUBYAS —an acronym for First Usual Brand Young Adult Smokers. The company's own research in the 1980s revealed a noteworthy behavior among smokers: the brand that they use when they first become regular smokers is the brand that smokers stay with for years. There is a great deal of brand loyalty among smokers.

Third, prior to the campaign, about 2 to 3 percent of smokers under the age of eighteen named Camel as their brand. By 1989, a year into the campaign, Camel's share of underage smokers had risen to 8.1 percent and within a few years it had grown to at least 13 percent. During this same period, Camel's share of the adult market barely moved from its 4 percent market share.

The campaign succeeded in resurrecting the moribund Camel brand. But it also managed to create an icon recognizable to even the youngest children. Two studies, one by an independent researcher and one company funded, found that children as young as three to six easily recognize Joe Camel and know that he is associated with cigarettes. The company's researcher found that children were as familiar with Joe Camel as they were with Ronald McDonald. This fact is significant because children this young get most of their product information from television advertising. But cigarettes have not been advertised on television since 1970.

The campaign was clearly very effective with the target group—the YAS smokers. But it was also effective with the younger, under eighteen smokers. . . .

Teenagers Can Easily Buy Cigarettes

The Camel campaign demonstrates how marketing and promotion targeted at younger tobacco users can also reach children and adolescents. And those young people who choose to smoke have easy access to the products. Tobacco products are among the most widely available consumer products in America, available in virtually every gas station, convenience store, drug store, and grocery store. And though every state in the country prohibits the sale of cigarettes to those who are underage, study after study demonstrates that these laws are widely ignored. Teenagers can purchase tobacco products with little effort— and they know it. A 1990 survey by the National Cancer Institute found that eight out of ten ninth graders said it would be easy for them to buy their own cigarettes. By some estimates, at least as many as 255 million packs are sold illegally to minors each year.

Younger smokers are more likely to buy their cigarettes from vending machines, where they can make their purchases quickly, often unnoticed by adults. The vending machine industry's own study found that thirteen-year-olds are eleven times more likely to buy cigarettes from vending machines than seventeen-year-olds. The 1994 Surgeon General's report examined nine studies on vending machine sales and found that underage persons were able to buy cigarettes 82 to 100 percent of the time.

> *"Joe Camel gave the company what it wanted: a new vehicle to reposition the Camel brand with more youth appeal."*

But the easy access does not stop with vending machines. Self-service displays allow buyers to help themselves to a pack of cigarettes or a can of smokeless with minimal contact with a sales clerk. This makes it easier for an underage person to buy tobacco products.

I've told you today that 90 percent of those who smoke began to do so as children and teenagers. I've told you that most of them become addicted and that seven out of ten wish they could quit. I've told you that the tobacco industry spends more than $5 billion a year to advertise and promote an addictive product and it uses cartoon characters, t-shirts and other gimmicks that appeal to children. I've told you that one company went so far as to develop a young adult smokers program which, intentional or not, increased cigarette sales to children.

Some may choose to ignore these facts. Some will continue to insist that the issue is an adult's freedom of choice. Nicotine addiction begins as a pediatric disease. Yet our society as a whole has done little to discourage this addiction in our youth. We must all recognize this fact and we must do more to discourage this addiction in our youth.

Measures to Reduce Teenage Addiction

A comprehensive and meaningful approach to preventing future generations of young people from becoming addicted to nicotine in tobacco is needed. Any such approach should first, reduce the many avenues of easy access to tobacco products available to children and teenagers; second, get the message to our young people that nicotine is addictive and that tobacco products pose serious health hazards—and not just for someone else; and third, reduce the powerful imagery in tobacco advertising and promotion that encourages young people to begin using tobacco products.

These types of actions have been advocated by many public health experts and organizations, including most recently the Institute of Medicine, which issued a report on smoking and children in 1994. And a 1995 public opinion poll sponsored by the Robert Wood Johnson Foundation showed widespread public support for measures to reduce smoking by young people. . . .

Of course we all want freedom for our children. But not the freedom to make irreversible decisions in childhood that result in devastating health consequences for the future. Addiction is freedom denied. We owe it to our children to help them enter adulthood free from addiction. Our children are entitled to a lifetime of choices, not a lifelong addiction.

Curbs on Cigarette Advertising Can Prevent Teenage Smoking

by Bill Clinton

About the author: *Bill Clinton is president of the United States.*

Editor's Note: The following viewpoint is excerpted from a news conference given by President Bill Clinton on August 10, 1995, in which he announced an executive order to impose regulations on cigarette sales and advertising.

Today I am announcing broad executive action to protect the young people of the United States from the awful dangers of tobacco.

The Dangers of Teenage Smoking

Over the years, we have learned more and more about the dangers of addictive substances to our young people. In the 60s and 70s, we came to realize the threat drugs posed to young Americans. In the 80s we came to grips with the awful problem of drunk driving among young people. It is time to take a third step to free our teenagers from addiction and dependency.

Adults are capable of making their own decisions about whether to smoke. But we all know that children are especially susceptible to the deadly temptation of tobacco and its skillful marketing. Today, and every day this year, 3,000 young people will begin to smoke; 1,000 of them ultimately will die of cancer, emphysema, heart disease and other diseases caused by smoking. That's more than a million vulnerable young people a year being hooked on nicotine that ultimately could kill them.

Therefore, by executive authority, I will restrict sharply the advertising, promotion, distribution and marketing of cigarettes to teenagers.

I do this on the basis of the best available scientific evidence—the findings of the American Medical Association, the American Cancer Society, the Ameri-

From Bill Clinton's news conference on his tobacco order, August 10, 1995, as transcribed by Federal Information Systems Corp. and reprinted in the *New York Times*, August 11, 1995.

can Heart Association, the American Lung Association, the Centers for Disease Control and Prevention. Fourteen months of study by the Food and Drug Administration confirms what we all know: Cigarettes and smokeless tobacco are harmful, highly addictive and aggressively marketed to our young people.

The evidence is overwhelming, and the threat is immediate.

Our children face a health crisis that is getting worse. One-third more eighth graders and one-quarter more tenth graders are smoking today than four years ago [in 1991]. One out of five high school seniors is a daily smoker. We need to act, and we must act now, before another generation of Americans is condemned to fight a difficult and grueling personal battle with an addiction that will cost millions of them their lives.

Adults make their own decisions about whether or not to smoke. Relatively few people start to smoke past their teens. Many adults have quit. Many have tried and failed.

But we all know that teenagers are especially susceptible to pressures—pressure to the manipulation of mass media advertising, the pressure of the seduction of skilled marketing campaigns aimed at exploiting their insecurities and uncertainties about life.

When Joe Camel tells young children that smoking is cool, when billboards tell teens that smoking will lead to true romance, when Virginia Slims tells adolescents that cigarettes may make them thin and glamorous, then our children need our wisdom, our guidance and our experience.

Steps to Stop Sales to Teenagers

We are their parents, and it is put to us to protect them. So, today I am authorizing the Food and Drug Administration to initiate a broad series of steps all designed to stop sales and marketing of cigarettes and smokeless tobacco to children.

As a result, the following steps will be taken:

First, young people will have to prove their age, with an ID card, to buy cigarettes.

> *"We all know that children are especially susceptible to the deadly temptation of tobacco and its skillful marketing."*

Second, cigarette vending machines, which circumvent any ban on sales to kids, will be prohibited.

Third, schools and playgrounds will be free of tobacco advertising on billboards in their neighborhoods.

Fourth, images such as Joe Camel will not appear on billboards or in ads in publications that reach substantial numbers of children and teens.

Fifth, teens won't be targeted by any marketing gimmicks, ranging from single cigarette sales to T-shirts, gym bags and sponsorship of sporting events.

And finally, the tobacco industry must fund and implement an annual $150 million campaign aimed at stopping teens from smoking through educational efforts.

Now, these are all commonsense steps. They don't ban smoking; they don't bar advertising. We do not, in other words, seek to address activities that sell, that seek to sell, cigarettes only to adults. We are stepping in to protect those who need our help, our vulnerable young people. And the evidence of increasing smoking in the last few years is plain and compelling.

Now, nobody much likes Government regulation, and I would prefer it if we could have done this in some other way.

The only other way I can think of is if Congress were to write these restrictions into law. They could do that, and if they do, this rule could become unnecessary. But it is wrong to believe that we can take a voluntary approach to this problem. . . .

Less smoking means less cancer, less illness, longer lives, a stronger America. Acting together we can make a difference. With this concerted plan targeted at those practices that especially prey upon our children, we can save lives, and we will.

To those who produce and market cigarettes, I say today, take responsibility for your actions. Sell your products only to adults. Draw the line on children. Show by your deeds as well as your words that you recognize that it is wrong, as well as illegal, to hook one million children a year on tobacco.

Regulation of Tobacco Marketing Will Not Prevent Teenage Smoking

by *The Economist*

About the author: The Economist *is a liberal British weekly news magazine.*

Here at *The Economist*, people who want to light a cigarette do so where they will not bother others. That is as it should be: smoking is smelly and, to the sensitive, annoying. But that is as far as this liberal (in the British sense) newspaper goes. In America a century ago, Mary Walker, a decorated Civil War nurse who raged against "evil nicotine", went about the streets using her furled umbrella to bat cigarettes from the lips of unsuspecting smokers. The August 1995 announcement by the Clinton administration that it would mount a heavy-handed campaign against smoking by teenagers is, alas, more in her tradition than in ours.

Measures to Restrict Cigarette Advertising

The Clintonites have decided to regulate nicotine as an addictive and harmful drug (which it is). Beginning from that premise, they would, among other things, require cigarette advertisements on billboards and in most magazines to be in youth-unfriendly black and white, with no pictures; ban cigarette brands from sponsoring entertainment or sporting events; and require tobacco companies to spend $150 million a year on anti-smoking campaigns aimed at teenagers. For present purposes, leave aside, as many European countries have done, the conflicts these measures create with freedom of speech. That apart, does this new "war" on teenage smoking make practical sense?

It is certainly true that smoking is hazardous to the health. So is eating lots of fat, or riding motorcycles (which are 16 times deadlier than cars). A liberal society normally lets people take foolish risks, provided the risk-takers pay the costs and assume them knowingly. In the case of smoking, they do. Kip Viscusi, an economist at America's Duke University, recently had the most comprehensive look to date at who pays for America's tobacco habit. He concludes, as others have done, that smokers pay their own way. What they cost in medical bills, fires and so on, they more than repay in pensions they do not live to collect and nursing-home care they never use. Tobacco taxes in America are now more than high enough to cover any residual costs of second-hand smoke. Far from harming society, American smokers hurt only themselves.

Dangerous Choices

But surely the case is different with teenagers? Apparently not. Most people—smokers and non-smokers—overestimate the dangers of smoking by a factor of two or more. Teenagers, it turns out, have an even more exaggerated view of smoking's perils than grown-ups do. Even among American eight-year-olds, 97 percent know that smoking causes cancer and shortens life, and the vast majority know it is hard to stop. If teenagers smoke, that is not because they are ignorant. Perhaps their judgment about smoking is poorer than their elders—but even that is unclear: Mr Viscusi finds that teenagers are as likely to act, or not act, on their knowledge about smoking as are adults.

Requiring drug companies—including cigarette makers—to divulge the harmful effects of their products is a good thing. So is forbidding sales to minors, who should have their parents' permission to smoke. However, spending millions of scarce dollars to educate people who demonstrably do not need further educating is rather less sensible. Still, that is no more foolish than many other things governments do, such as subsidising opera tickets and rich farmers. If Washington wants to crusade against smoking, why not?

Washington is not proposing to spend Washington's money. It proposes, rather, to force tobacco companies to spend in its stead. A basic principle of good government is that public benefits should be paid for from public funds. If Washington wants an anti-cholesterol campaign, it should not require ice-cream companies to finance one. For good reason: governments spend others' money far more profligately than money they raise themselves. Just watch. If Mr Clinton is forced to dig into the Treasury's pockets rather than reaching into the tobacco companies', that $150 million anti-smoking campaign will never happen. Feeding the poor, curing AIDS and plugging the deficit will rightly be deemed more important.

If it wants to do something useful, America would be far better off bringing reason to its zanily incoherent policies on recreational drugs of

> *"Does this new 'war' on teenage smoking make practical sense?"*

all kinds. Tobacco growers enjoy government support while marijuana growers, whose crop is no more dangerous or addictive, are thrown into prison. Instead of treating cigarettes like other addictive drugs, let America treat other addictive drugs like cigarettes and alcohol: publicise the risks, tax the users, and ban sales to minors. Then leave people to make their mistakes, and to learn.

Restricting Tobacco Advertising Will Not Affect Teenage Smoking

by the *Wall Street Journal*

About the author: *The* Wall Street Journal *is a daily business newspaper.*

President Bill Clinton has finally found an industry he can bash without it being hazardous to his political health. In the eyes of most voters, tobacco companies are true villains, unlike the drug companies he tried to blame for low vaccination rates among preschoolers, or the health insurers he wanted to take the fall for the problems of our health care system. So the President's new campaign will score political points, but will it help reduce smoking?

Smoking Has Declined, Except Among Teenagers

To start with, Mr. Clinton and the Food and Drug Administration's David Kessler are coming late to the party. In 1965, the year after the Surgeon General's report linking smoking and cancer, 45% of Americans smoked. As of 1995, that figure has dwindled to roughly 25%—and practically all of them say they want to stop. What happened in the intervening years, of course, was the Great American Smokeout. Americans educated themselves on the dangers of smoking; the government helped, by issuing warnings and passing state and local laws, but the most important ingredient was a change in cultural attitudes toward smoking.

It was a change in what is called, in the current buzzword, civil society. Today, as every remaining smoker knows, it is virtually impossible to light up in public and more and more difficult to do so in private. Smoking is now an activity in which one engages in the sanctity of one's own home or in the Great Outdoors, where refugees from smoke-free zones flee when they need to feed their habit.

But while smoking rates continue to fall among adults, teen smoking is a different matter. The University of Michigan's annual survey of high school students, out in July 1995, shows a sharp increase in the percentage of teens who smoke (defined as smoking any cigarettes in the past thirty days). The sharpest increase is among eighth-graders, an astonishing 18.6% of whom smoke; the smoking rate among high school seniors is now 31.2%, higher than the adult rate. The Michigan researchers put the increases down principally to two factors: teens' unrealistically low perception of the dangers of smoking and a weakening of peer norms against smoking. One fascinating bit of information from various studies of teen smokers is that black teens are far less likely to smoke than whites or Hispanics; anecdotal evidence shows black adolescents tend to think of smoking as a "white thing." It's probably no coincidence that a number of black urban churches sponsor strong anti-smoking campaigns.

Proposed Restrictions Will Not Work

The question is: At this point, what does Washington have to contribute? The White House proposes to bar cigarette sales to under-eighteen-year-olds and require ID checks. It asks for federal laws banning vending-machine sales. It proposes restrictions on advertising—no brand-name sponsorship of athletic events; no billboard ads within 1,000 feet of schools; black-and-white, text-only ads in publications aimed at teens. And it asks that the tobacco companies fork over $150 million a year in anti-smoking educational materials aimed at children.

In principle Mr. Clinton has a point: Surely cigarette smoking is bad for you and for society, and public policy should seek to minimize it. Yet his specific proposals would be further government-imposed nuisances, whose chief direct effect will be to make millionaires of a few more lawyers. Only a small percentage of cigarette sales are through vending

> *"The most important ingredient [in the decline of smoking in America] was a change in cultural attitudes toward smoking."*

machines, for example, and the FBI is not going to stake out delis to see if they ID youthful-looking customers. The impact of these measures, like the ones before, would have to be through using the law to promote education and moral suasion.

The Government's Role in Reducing Drug Use

The big problem with Mr. Clinton's plan is that it's going to be run by a federal government that doesn't currently have much moral capital. Mr. Kessler has the scientific and moral standing of a grandstander. And in setting out to tackle nicotine, Mr. Clinton's Administration has done no swell job of regulating harder drugs. It has abandoned Nancy Reagan's "Just Say No" campaign of the '80s in favor of concentrating on hard-core drug users. The use of hard drugs among teens dropped under the earlier approach, and is now increasing. Indeed, we suspect the increase in both tobacco and drugs reflects a moral aura to which the

White House has contributed no little.

The way to keep kids off cigarettes is the same way to keep them off marijuana or cocaine: Persuade them that it's a bad idea—that in the long run cigarettes kill and in the short run are a disgusting habit. While there certainly is a role for government—particularly in setting the moral tone—such a campaign is probably better left to civic culture. If President Clinton really wants to curb smoking instead of merely making political points, he might call tobacco to the attention of the private groups dealing rather well, thank you, with drunken driving, TV violence and gangsta rap.

Teenage Smoking Can Be Prevented Without FDA Regulation of Cigarettes

by James J. Morgan

About the author: *James J. Morgan is president and chief executive officer of Philip Morris U.S.A., a Richmond, Virginia-based cigarette manufacturer.*

In May 1996, President Bill Clinton spoke to a group of high school students in Woodbridge, New Jersey, about tobacco. The president directed some of his comments to the tobacco industry. "Join with us," he said, "do not stay outside of and apart from this debate."

A Proposal to Restrict Teenage Use of Tobacco

The following week, Philip Morris U.S.A. and the United States Tobacco Co. accepted the president's challenge. Together, we proposed federal legislation to address the issue of underage tobacco use.

This initiative builds on our commitment that minors should not use or even have access to tobacco products. We have offered this comprehensive plan in the hope that all sides in the debate will work toward our common goal: preventing underage tobacco use.

Everyone agrees that kids shouldn't use tobacco. And reasonable people agree that adults should be able to make a personal choice about whether to smoke. Our proposal would make it impossible for anyone to legally obtain any tobacco product without a face-to-face transaction where age could be verified.

Our advertising is focused on adult smokers only and meant to influence their brand choices. We do not believe that advertising causes anyone, including minors, to start smoking. Nevertheless, we're willing to accept new restrictions on our advertising and promotion in order to put politics aside and act now to address this problem. The legislative plan we have announced includes, for example, a ban on non-tobacco-related items, such as hats and T-shirts, that carry

James J. Morgan, "A Plan to Keep Kids from Smoking," *Los Angeles Times*, June 13, 1996. Reprinted by permission of the author.

tobacco brand names. Also included are bans on mass transit advertising and outdoor advertising within 1,000 feet of elementary and secondary schools and public playgrounds and even a ban on vending machines.

The law that we want to see enacted would have tough regulation, oversight and enforcement measures at the federal and state levels. The Department of Health and Human Services would have oversight over sales and distribution restrictions, with enforcement by the Department of Justice and the states. The Federal Trade Commission, which has many years of experience in tobacco regulation, would enforce the advertising and marketing restrictions.

Tobacco manufacturers would be subject to fines of up to $50,000 for violations and would contribute $250 million over five years to help pay for enforcement and related programs.

Arguments Against FDA Regulation

Many of the elements of our proposal parallel those of the Food and Drug Administration, but do so without creating a huge new bureaucracy or unreasonably limiting the rights of adults to make their own choices. The FDA's mission is to ensure the safety and efficacy of the nation's food, drugs and medical devices, but it has said it would never find cigarettes "safe and effective" under food and drug laws. That is why we believe FDA regulation of tobacco raises the specter of new restrictions on sales to adults and eventually to prohibition of tobacco products.

"Reasonable people agree that adults should be able to make a personal choice about whether to smoke."

We believe that only Congress can make such a monumental decision as prohibiting the sale of tobacco products to adults. The FDA does not and should not have that power. On more than twenty occasions, Congress has declined to give the FDA authority over cigarettes. And the FDA historically has taken the position that it does not have such authority—a position that the courts have upheld.

The president has stated his preference for a federal legislative approach over a long, complicated, contentious regulatory proceeding or years of litigation. As he put it, "We believe it's better to have the companies come forward and ask for legislation, and the FDA has made perfectly clear that they will stop their efforts to impose regulations if we can have a joint agreement on a legislative solution."

The Real Aim of Tobacco Regulations

In rejecting our plan, some of our critics have revealed their true aim: using FDA regulation to create a "smoke-free society" where adults may not use tobacco. It's time for more reasonable people to come together to fight underage tobacco use.

President Clinton asked the tobacco industry to propose a legislative solution to the youth smoking issue. We've put one on the table. It's a serious, comprehensive plan with teeth. It can become law quickly, avoiding years of legal conflict. And it addresses the issue of underage tobacco use squarely and fairly, without unreasonably threatening the rights of adults.

One thing is certain: If we argue and delay, we will have problems, not progress. If we work together to fight the problem and not one another, we can make a difference. Let's get started.

Bibliography

Books

Gayle M. Boyd, Jan Howard, and Robert A. Zucker, eds.	*Alcohol Problems Among Adolescents: Current Directions in Prevention Research*. Hillsdale, NJ: Lawrence Erlbaum, 1995.
Oscar Gary Bukstein	*Adolescent Substance Abuse: Assessment, Prevention, and Treatment*. New York: Wiley, 1995.
Donna Gaines	*Teenage Wasteland: Suburbia's Dead End Kids*. New York: Pantheon, 1991.
Stanton A. Glantz et al.	*The Cigarette Papers*. Berkeley and Los Angeles: University of California Press, 1996.
Mark S. Gold	*Cocaine*. New York: Plenum Medical, 1993.
Mark S. Gold	*Tobacco*. New York: Plenum Medical, 1995.
Thomas P. Gullotta, Gerald R. Adams, and Raymond Montemayor, eds.	*Substance Misuse in Adolescence*. Thousand Oaks, CA: Sage, 1995.
Leigh A. Henderson and William J. Glass, eds.	*LSD: Still with Us After All These Years*. New York: Lexington Books, 1994.
Philip J. Hilts	*Smokescreen: The Truth Behind the Tobacco Industry Cover-Up*. Reading, MA: Addison-Wesley, 1996.
George S. Howard and Peter E. Nathan, eds.	*Alcohol Use and Misuse by Young Adults*. Notre Dame, IN: University of Notre Dame Press, 1994.
Richard Kluger	*Ashes to Ashes: America's Hundred-Year Cigarette War, the Public Health, and the Unabashed Triumph of Philip Morris*. New York: Knopf, 1996.
Barbara S. Lynch and Richard J. Bonnie, eds.	*Growing Up Tobacco Free: Preventing Nicotine Addiction in Children and Youths*. Washington, DC: Institute of Medicine, National Academy Press, 1994.
Mike Males	*The Scapegoat Generation: America's War Against Adolescents*. Monroe, ME: Common Courage Press, 1996.
Elizabeth Wurzel	*Prozac Nation: Young and Depressed in America*. Boston: Houghton Mifflin, 1994.

Periodicals

Jerry Adler	"The Endless Binge," *Newsweek*, December 19, 1994.

Bibliography

J.M. Balkin	"Give Them Liberty to Give Us Death?" *Washington Monthly*, October 1995.
James Bovard	"Unsafe at Any Speed," *American Spectator*, April 1996.
Lonnie R. Bristow	"Protecting Youth from the Tobacco Industry," *Vital Speeches of the Day*, March 15, 1994.
Bob Cohn and Bill Turque	"Firing Up the Politics of Teen Smoking," *Newsweek*, August 21, 1995.
Congressional Digest	"Tobacco Use Among Young People," May 1994.
Lyle Deniston	"Should Cigarette Ads Be Banned?" *American Journalism Review*, November 1994.
Jeff Elliott	"Just Say Nonsense," *Washington Monthly*, May 1993.
Charles Gandee	"Under the Influence," *Vogue*, March 1994.
Elizabeth Gleick	"Out of the Mouths of Babes," *Time*, August 21, 1995.
Christine Gorman	"Higher Education: Crocked on Campus," *Time*, December 19, 1994.
Monika Guttman	"Why Teens Refuse to Give Up Smoking," *U.S. News & World Report*, August 7, 1995.
Kendall Hamilton	"Dusting for Kids' Dope," *Newsweek*, April 24, 1995.
Peter Jaret	"Young Women and Alcohol," *Glamour*, April 1995.
Tamara Jones	"Out of Control," *Reader's Digest*, May 1995.
Michael Krantz	"Seagram's on the Box," *Time*, June 24, 1996.
John Leland	"A Risky Rx for Fun," *Newsweek*, October 30, 1995.
David Lipsky	"The Hard-Core Curriculum," *Rolling Stone*, October 19, 1995.
Martin E. Marty	"The Curse of the Drinking Class," *Christian Century*, February 22, 1995.
Sylvester Monroe	"D.A.R.E. Bedeviled," *Time*, October 17, 1994.
Timothy C. Morgan	"The Invisible Addiction," *Christianity Today*, April 8, 1996.
Rodney Smith	"Puffin' for Proofs of Purchase," *Z Magazine*, July/August 1995.
Fara Warner	"Liquor Industry Tackles Teenage Drinking," *Wall Street Journal*, June 30, 1995.
Henry Wechsler et al.	"Health and Behavioral Consequences of Binge Drinking in College," *JAMA: Journal of the American Medical Association*, December 7, 1994. Available from 515 N. State St., Chicago, IL 60610.

Organizations to Contact

The editors have compiled the following list of organizations concerned with the issues debated in this book. The descriptions are derived from materials provided by the organizations. All have publications or information available for interested readers. The list was compiled on the date of publication of the present volume; names, addresses, fax and phone numbers, and internet addresses may change. Be aware that many organizations take several weeks or longer to respond to inquiries, so allow as much time as possible.

American College of Sports Medicine
PO Box 1440
Indianapolis, IN 46206-1440
(317) 637-9200
fax: (317) 634-7817

This group of physicians and health specialists is the largest sports medicine organization in the world. It sponsors scientific research on the abuse of steroids and other drugs in sports. Its publications include the pamphlets *Alcohol in Sports*, *Youth Fitness*, and *Anabolic Steroids and Athletes*.

American Council on Science and Health (ACSH)
1995 Broadway, 2nd Fl.
New York, NY 10023-5860
(212) 362-7044
fax: (212) 362-4919

ACSH is a consumer education group composed of physicians, scientists, and policy advisers. It is concerned with educating consumers about health, lifestyle, and environmental issues and the safety of foods and pharmaceuticals. The council publishes the quarterly magazine *Priorities* and special reports on the hazards of smoking.

Americans for Nonsmokers' Rights
2530 San Pablo Ave., Suite J
Berkeley, CA 94701
(510) 841-3032
fax: (510) 841-7702

This antismoking organization lobbies local governments to adopt smoke-free indoor air laws. Its educational arm, the American Nonsmokers' Rights Foundation, publishes tobacco education and smoking prevention materials for adolescents, including *The Tobacco Industry Has a Bad Habit* and *How to Butt In! Teens Take Action Guidebook*.

Center on Addiction and Substance Abuse (CASA)
Columbia University
152 W. 57th St.
New York, NY 10019
(212) 841-5200

CASA conducts research on drug abuse and prevention among young people. It publishes periodic reports, such as "Rethinking Rites of Passage," on drinking and substance abuse among high school and college students, young women, and teenagers.

Drug Policy Foundation
4455 Connecticut Ave. NW, Suite B-500
Washington, DC 20008-2302
(202) 537-5005
fax: (202) 537-3007

The foundation is dedicated to studying alternatives to the war on drugs. It supports legalization of drug use, though not for minors. It publishes the quarterly *Drug Policy Letter*.

Drugs and Data Center and Clearinghouse
1600 Research Blvd.
Rockville, MD 20850
(800) 732-3277

The clearinghouse distributes the publications of the U.S. Department of Justice, the Drug Enforcement Administration, and other related federal agencies.

Institute for Social Research
University of Michigan
Ann Arbor, MI 48109-1399
(313) 747-4416

The institute conducts the annual Monitoring the Future survey, which gathers data on drug use (including smoking) and attitudes toward drugs among eighth-, tenth-, and twelfth-grade students. Results of the survey are published by the **National Institute on Drug Abuse (NIDA)**.

Narcotics Anonymous (NA)
World Service Office—USA
PO Box 9999
Van Nuys, CA 91409
(818) 773-9999
fax: (818) 700-0700

World Service Office—Canada
150 Britannia Rd. East, Unit 21
Mississauga, ON L4Z 2A4
CANADA
(416) 507-0100
fax: (416) 507-0101

NA is a twelve-step program that focuses on overcoming the disease of addiction. It publishes *Narcotics Anonymous*, the basic text of the twelve-step process, and numerous pamphlets, such as *Youth and Recovery*.

National Association of State Alcohol and Drug Abuse Directors (NASADAD)
444 N. Capitol St. NW, Suite 642
Washington, DC 20001
(202) 783-6868
fax: (202) 783-2704

NASADAD assists the federal and state governments in the development of alcohol and drug abuse prevention and treatment programs throughout the United States. It publishes the newsletter *State Substance Abuse Quarterly* and the annual *State Resources and Services Related to Alcohol and Drug Abuse Problems.*

National Clearinghouse for Alcohol and Drug Information
PO Box 2345
Rockville, MD 20847-2345
(800) 729-6686

The clearinghouse distributes publications of the U.S. Department of Health and Human Services, the **National Institute on Drug Abuse**, and other federal agencies concerned with alcohol and drug abuse.

National Council on Alcoholism and Drug Dependence (NCADD)
12 W. 21st St.
New York, NY 10010
(212) 206-6770
fax: (212) 645-1690

NCADD is a volunteer health organization that, in addition to helping individuals overcome addictions, advises the federal government on drug and alcohol policies and develops substance abuse prevention and education programs for youth. It publishes fact sheets, such as *Youth and Alcohol*, and pamphlets, such as *Who's Got the Power? You . . . or Drugs?*

National Criminal Justice Reference Service (NCJRS)
U.S. Department of Justice
Rockville, MD 20849-6000
(800) 851-3420

The NCJRS distributes publications of the U.S. Department of Justice, the National Institute of Justice, and other federal agencies. For a nominal fee it can provide a bibliography on any topic related to criminal justice, juvenile justice, or substance abuse.

National Institute on Drug Abuse (NIDA)
U.S. Department of Health and Human Services
5600 Fishers Ln.
Rockville, MD 20857
(301) 443-6245

NIDA supports and conducts research on drug abuse—including the yearly Monitoring the Future Survey—in order to improve addiction prevention, treatment, and policy efforts. It publishes the bimonthly *NIDA Notes* newsletter, periodic *NIDA Capsules* fact sheets, and a catalog of research reports and public education materials, such as *Marijuana: Facts for Teens.*

New Jersey Alcohol/Drug Resource Center and Clearinghouse
Smithers Hall, Busch Campus
Rutgers University
Piscataway, NJ 08855-0969
(908) 445-0792
fax: (908) 445-0790

The clearinghouse provides technical assistance and resources to schools, communities, and state agencies for the development of alcohol and drug abuse prevention education programs. It publishes periodic fact sheets, such as *Facts On: Adolescent Substance Abuse.*

Reason Foundation
3415 S. Sepulveda Blvd., Suite 400
Los Angeles, CA 90034
(310) 391-2245

This public policy organization researches contemporary social and political problems and promotes libertarian philosophy and free-market principles. It publishes the monthly *Reason* magazine, which contains articles and editorials critical of the war on drugs and smoking regulation.

Volunteers of America
3939 N. Causeway Blvd., Suite 400
Metairie, LA 70002
(800) 899-0089
Internet: http://www.voa.org

This Catholic service organization offers counseling and educational programs for youth, alcoholics, and drug abusers. It publishes *The Spirit of America*, a curriculum guide for teaching children the value of community service.

Wisconsin Clearinghouse for Prevention Resources
1552 University Ave.
Madison, WI 53705
(800) 322-1468
fax: (608) 262-6346
Internet: http://www.uhs.wisc.edu/wch/

The clearinghouse produces and distributes prevention materials for schools, communities, colleges and universities, prevention agencies, health care settings, and others. Books, videos, posters, pamphlets, and software are available through their catalog on a wide variety of prevention topics: alcohol and other drug abuse, violence prevention and anger management, conflict resolution, alternatives, self-esteem, teen pregnancy, and sexually transmitted diseases.

Index